All to the Glory of GOD

Ken Collier & Ken Hay

Taylors, South Carolina

All to the Glory of God

Ken Collier and Ken Hay

All Scripture is quoted from the Authorized King James Version.

Associate Editors/Authors: Joel and JoAnn Brighton

Cover design by Craig Stouffer

Page design and layout by Kelley Moore

Taylors, SC 29687

ISBN 978-0-9815235-5-2

About the Title "All to the Glory of God"

Two years before THE WILDS was begun, Dr. Ken Hay, the founder of the ministry, took part in an awards' banquet in Charlotte, North Carolina. His brother-in-law, Phil Starr, who was in charge of the banquet, placed a banner at the front and over the podium that declared, "*Whether therefore ye eat or drink or whatsoever ye do; do all to the glory of God* (1 Corinthians 10:31)." Ken Hay was captivated by the simple message that encompassed every motive, thought, action, and word in a Christian's life. Is it any wonder that the camp he founded is built on that verse?

Three times a day, at every meal during full camp days, for over forty years, this verse has been quoted. On rare occasions when the program man has failed to lead campers in the verse before the meal, campers and staff, almost in panic, have insisted that it be quoted after the meal. Over half a million campers and staff members have had etched in their minds the real purpose of life on earth through this verse and through this place.

Are you living your life to bring glory to the One who created you and who loved you enough to die for you? Do all to the glory of God!

CONTENTS

FOREWORD

Rare is the opportunity for an outsider to observe the development of an idea from its inception to a multifaceted ministry influencing hundreds of thousands of people for the glory of God. It has been my privilege to be one who has watched with gratitude and amazement the development of a staff, the construction of a facility that is outstanding, and the maintaining of the solid biblical mission of THE WILDS Christian Association.

THE WILDS had a major impact on our early ministry and continues to be a model forty years later. Lessons learned from Dr. Hay and others are innumerable. Pastors and youth workers from the past often heard me say, "To be a good youth pastor, you need to know how to drive a bus and get your young people to THE WILDS." The impact of THE WILDS on our youth ministry in Roseville, Michigan, will be revealed in eternal fruit.

My experience is a microcosm of numerous other leaders whose teens, families, pastors, singles, and even senior saints have grown in their knowledge of God and in their commitment to the cause of Christ. Each local church touched by THE WILDS is strengthened.

How can THE WILDS be described? Some of the characteristics that automatically spring to mind are excellence, servant attitude, biblical conviction, passionate preaching, personal touch, evangelism, sacrificial abandonment to God's cause, balance, clear God focus, and most of all, a desire to glorify God.

From the beginning, the mindset of the leaders was to present a proper opinion of our God in every phase of the ministry. Even during something as common as mealtime, one is reminded of that objective as the theme verse is quoted three times a day. 1 Corinthians 10:31 declares, "Whether therefore ye eat, or drink, or whatsoever ye do, do all to the glory of God."

THE WILDS Christian Camp and Conference Center has a heritage that is rich, a heavenly mission that is ongoing, and a holy calling to be steadfast, unmovable, and always abounding in the work of the Lord.

May God be glorified through THE WILDS ministry until we awake in His likeness!

Dr. Les Ollila, Chancellor
Northland International University
Dunbar, Wisconsin

ACKNOWLEDGEMENTS

The beauty and blessing of THE WILDS is that no single individual or group is responsible for bringing THE WILDS into existence. All thanks and all glory goes to God and our Savior, the Lord Jesus Christ. *"For of him, and through him, and to him, are all things: to whom be glory for ever. Amen"* (Romans 11:36). We believe He would be pleased that we give special thanks to the following people:

- Ken and Diane Hay for their vision in seeing the need for a camp to touch the lives of families and young people and for stepping out in faith to meet this great need.
- Joe Henson and Carl Blyth along with Ken Hay for sacrificially laying the foundation for the organization that has become THE WILDS.
- The late Walter Fremont for his years of earnest prayers to God to raise up a camp like THE WILDS and then for his continued prayers and precious friendship to this ministry.
- The Board of Directors past and present for exercising trust and giving guidance through the years.
- Thousands of summer staff members who have been the backbone of the ministry and who have sacrificed to present the Truth of God with the love of God so lives can be changed to the glory of God.
- Weekend staff who have faithfully attended to the needs of our campers during weekend camps and conferences.

- Thousands of volunteers who have hammered, sawed, nailed, raked, chipped, cleaned, served food, organized banquets, filled tables, stuffed letters, made phone calls, repaired screens, dug trenches, manned golf tournaments, and done a thousand other things.
- Our financial Sustainers, both local churches and individuals, who have faithfully supported us like clockwork, standing by the ministry with faithful prayers and gifts through the years.
- Full-time staff who have sacrificially served, been faithful and loyal while laughing and loving everyday in a cause that is bigger than any one of them.
- Parents who have believed in this ministry and have proven it by allowing their children to serve on staff or come as campers to THE WILDS.
- Campers past and present who love THE WILDS and have made it their camp.
- Mike, Melody, Justin, and Angela who gave their ultimate best *to the glory of God* serving at THE WILDS.
- Joel and Jo Ann Brighton who spent literally hundreds of hours interviewing friends of THE WILDS in preparation for this book, served as the associate editors/authors, and who, themselves, have counted the cost through the trying of their faith (see appendix A).
- The committee who served sacrificially to produce this book: Joel and Jo Ann Brighton, Ken and Diane Hay, Ken Collier, Karen Cleary, Cal Mair, and Barbara Leatherwood.
- These who gave their expertise to help in the production of this book: Craig Stouffer, Michelle Adams, Vickie Ebner, Nancy Lohr, and Kelley Moore.

Section One

"THE LORD WAS THERE!"

This statement of a Christian man who attended the groundbreaking is not wholly correct theologically. "The Lord **is** there" is much more accurate. In context, though, he was just making a statement that he was aware of the presence of God at that one event in the history of THE WILDS. "The Lord was there" can also be said of every event that unfolded one after the other in those beginning days of THE WILDS. God orchestrated the cast of diverse characters who came onto the scene giving prayer, advice, information, caution, and optimism. God used a teenager on a hiking trail. He used a realtor who recalled seeing an intriguing piece of property. He used an artist who suggested an innovative name for a camp. He used men and women who had been impacted by the institution of camping. God called them in, one at a time, to add their part to His creative plan to bring about THE WILDS.

God also used obstacles to test the resolve of God's people. He used a nest of yellow jackets to bring near panic. He used nearly impassable logging roads to test ingenuity. He used a lack of finances to test faith. He used a previously signed contract on a property to test dependency. He used plumbing, electrical, and water problems to test resoluteness. He used the weakness of men to show Himself powerful. God orchestrated every person and every detail to do His will. You can rejoice as you read of these early days of a fledgling ministry, because it is evident that "the Lord was there!"

Chapter One

A Man—A Prayer—A Dinner—A Dream

WHETHER THEREFORE YE EAT, OR DRINK,
OR WHATSOEVER YE DO, DO ALL TO THE GLORY OF GOD.

1 CORINTHIANS 10:31

God did not need this place called THE WILDS in order to accomplish His work. But how many people across this country—and the world—are glad that He chose to use it? The Lord could accomplish His wonderful work without the use of men, but He chooses to use willing, gifted men and women who will give the glory to Him.

THE WILDS in the eyes of the founders *is not a personality-centered ministry*—never has been and never should be. Ken Hay, one of the founders, has worn that statement out. The thousands of staff members who have heard it over and over would never in a million years dispute it. Yet God does choose men to begin faith-filled ventures for His glory, and He chose Ken Hay and his supportive wife,

Diane, for a special task . . . that of being the driving force responsible for founding THE WILDS.

A Burdened Man

The son of a pastor, Ken Hay was in and around camps all through his life, and he willingly accepted the call to serve God, where else but at a Christian camp, between his sophomore and junior years in high school. While God was doing His work in the young man's life in Oregon, He was also doing a similar work of grace in the heart of a certain young lady, Diane Mueller, in her native Kansas. Her decision, between her junior and senior years, was made in a Christian camp setting as well. God led these two westerners across the nation to Bob Jones University where they met, dated, and later became engaged, marrying in August of 1955.

It was the most natural thing throughout graduate school years, and later as members of the faculty at the university, for this active couple to use free summers in an outreach ministry they both loved, Christian camping. For thirteen summers between 1955 and 1968 (with the exception of 1959), the Hays worked in some type of summer camping ministry. He was an athletic director, a cleanup specialist, a camp evangelist, a program director, and a director. In his words, he was many times the "chief cook and bottle washer." She was a camp nurse (out of necessity), a craft director, a food service director, and "Mommy" to her own children as well as a substitute mommy to staff members in camps in Ohio, Georgia, Alabama, and South Carolina.

One of their summer ministry places was a little camp in Alabama where they met up with a young Ken Collier, who became like a son to them. Ken Collier, mentored by Ken Hay, would many years later be appointed Director of THE WILDS.

A PRAYER PARTNERSHIP

Ken Hay became fast friends with Dr. Walter Fremont, the Dean of the School of Education at Bob Jones University. Ken was named the first Director of the Institute of Christian Service. The young dean, Walt Fremont, mentored the even younger administrator, Ken, in the ministry. Meeting together two or three times a week for prayer in the Administration Building, the two prayed regularly for ten years that "somebody" would begin a quality camp in the Southeast to meet the needs of the burgeoning number of young people coming into their teenage years.

> God did not need this place called THE WILDS in order to accomplish His work.

Walt and Ken had much in common, including a deep-seated love for Christian camping. The Fremonts, like the Hays, were involved in camps in the summers. Both men had the conviction that camping was a dynamic tool in the hands of local churches for helping the teeming number of families and young people needing spiritual direction. Their prayers seemingly went unanswered for a time, but the object of that prayer—a camp in the Southeast—was simmering in the heart of the young visionary named Ken Hay. When it became apparent that his alma mater would not be able to start a camp, he facetiously remarked to Walt, "Well, I guess we'll have to start one ourselves."

His own prayer was soon to break upon his own life and the lives of thousands of others and alter them for eternity.

A DINNER, A DREAM, AND A PLAN

On May 24, 1967, two couples met for dinner in the home of Ken and Diane Hay. Gene and Lucille Fisher and Walt and Beverly Rumminger were getting better acquainted through the Hays. In the course of conversation one of the men mentioned he had recently purchased an investment property. The other had just received an inheritance that needed to be invested for the future. Between them that evening they formed the beginning of a corporation to build an apartment complex.

As Ken Hay sat listening taking in the conversation, he became restless in his spirit. Finally his heart was full enough to burst. He pounded his fist on the table and declared, "If you men have enough faith to go out and borrow money to start apartment buildings, then I should have enough faith to believe that God can help us start a camp!"

It was a sleepless night for Ken as he talked nonstop with the Lord and planned an entire campsite in his mind. In the morning he paid a visit to school president, Dr. Bob Jones III. Ken had heard that there was a businessman and student on campus, Carl Blyth, who was interested in camping. Dr. Jones said that this was true and that it was to be a point of the discussion at the next university board meeting. Ken, whose heart was now on fire with this vision, volunteered to be a part of the camping team if the college wanted to begin one.

Dr. Joe Henson, Chairman of the Division of Applied Science, was a like-minded Christian-camping enthusiast and became part of the team. Carl Blyth had access to a trust that might provide a portion of financing for the endeavor. Both the university and the fledgling camping group decided that it would be best to start the camp as a totally independent organization.

Now there was a small group of committed men in place; there was hope of some potential financial beginnings, but there was no campsite to call home.

A critical search—a critical decision—awaited the group.

In Their Own WORDS

I remember the many weeks my husband and Ken Hay met at noon to pray for someone to start a Christian ministry in this part of the country. When this goal came to fruition, there was rejoicing in our household. On our first trip to THE WILDS before any buildings were there and the road was rough and rugged, we incurred two flat tires. That did not dampen the thrill of seeing the answer to our prayers for a camp in the Southeast. THE WILDS has been a very important and vital part of our lives.

—Trudy Fremont (wife of the late Dr. Walter Fremont)

Chapter Two

FINDING A NAME AND A PROPERTY

DELIGHT THYSELF ALSO IN THE LORD; AND HE SHALL GIVE THEE THE DESIRES OF THINE HEART. COMMIT THY WAY UNTO THE LORD; TRUST ALSO IN HIM; AND HE SHALL BRING IT TO PASS.

PSALM 37:4–5

"POSSESSED" BEES?

In the fall of 1967, the property search began in earnest. Ken Hay saw the necessity of building close enough to a Christian college so that staff could be recruited for weekend camps. This foresight and insight became critical in the coming years.

The first property considered was a twenty-two hundred acre former hunting club called the Wing and Fin Club. Carl Blyth accompanied Ken on the excursion to view the expansive property. While walking the land, Carl stepped on a ground nest of yellow jackets and was stung numerous times. It quickly became apparent that he was deathly allergic to the venom. The isolation of the property and inaccessibility of a phone left Ken no choice but to get Carl to a hospital immediately and by any means. It was a frightening drive down U.S. Highway 25 with Ken driving at high speed and Carl, whose breathing was ragged and labored, begging him to go faster. They reached the hospital, and by God's grace, Carl's reaction to the stings broke in the wee hours of the morning.

But the men considered the situation with the bees. Were they sent to stop the whole procedure? Was it a warning from the Lord to stop the whole project or were the bees—in the jesting words of Ken Hay—"a group of demon-possessed bees" trying to stop God's work from going ahead? The men agreed that God had graciously given a test to their resolve—so full speed ahead.

This property could have been the place where the dream began and ended; instead it became the place of testing. In time this piece of land was eliminated from consideration, but only because God had a better location in another corner of the mountains.

"BEAUTIFUL PROPERTY, BUT WE'RE TOO LATE!"

A dear friend of THE WILDS ministry, Dr. Phil Smith, was camping with his family off of U.S. Highway 178 a few miles over the South Carolina border and into North Carolina. The owner of the campground, Bill Sager, owned five thousand acres of mountain property. Phil brought this information to Ken Hay's attention, who took a group of men to look at some of this acreage. Even Bill concluded after hearing the plans for the camp that his property was not suitable. Bill was a realtor, however, and his thoughts turned to an eight hundred plus-acre tract of land bordered by a one hundred thousand-acre wildlife preserve owned by Duke Power Company. The property was located off of that same Highway 178.

Bill Sager loaded the group into his jeep and turned off of Highway 178 onto a narrow, dusty gravel road with the quaint

Who in the world would want to bring his children down that road?

name of Old Toxaway Road, so named for the Toxaway Indian tribe which had in earlier days inhabited the area. They traveled the rutted, washboarded road for what seemed like twenty-five miles (actually only four and a half miles). Bill stopped the vehicle at the entrance of an old logging path in the vicinity of the present welcome sign. They hiked a mile to the site that would ultimately become the location for the Lodge—the center of camp. At that time the knoll was forty feet higher. Almost prophetically, Ken Hay remarked, "This is the perfect place for a camp lodge."

Try to imagine now that signature, welcoming Lodge located in another place. It would seem so strange that the Dining Hall and kitchen not be a stone's throw away from the center of camp where the mingled smells of deliciously prepared meals and fresh, hot rolls greet campers as they check in for the camp. Can you imagine the Ballfield with its myriad of activities and the cabins being anywhere other than down the signature one hundred thirteen steps? Even the placement of the familiar buildings and activities seem to be by God's direction. Virtually all of these envisioned building placements remain the same as the initial thinking on those first couple of visits.

In considering this piece of property, the men were troubled about the almost five-mile, graveled, primitive entrance. Who in the world would want to bring his children down that road? Certain questions are timeless. It is still on the minds of some the first time they make the trip to THE WILDS. The entrance gave every appearance of being at the very end of the world! The county—Transylvania County—was known as the "Land of Waterfalls," boasting over two hundred named waterfalls. It was rumored that there were beautiful waterfalls on this property that they were surveying. That fact would make this property a one in a million location. As the men prayed and puzzled, it was obvious that the property "near the end of the world" should not be eliminated from their property search and, in time, needed to be revisited.

After visiting up to forty different properties and eliminating many of them on the spot, several board members set out early on a Saturday morning to see the two most desirable properties left in the mix, the Old Toxaway property and another property only twenty miles away from Greenville, South Carolina, on U.S. Highway 276. The morning was hazy and overcast with rain falling intermittently. Still, the closer one looked at the Toxaway property, the more beautiful it became. As the men completed their survey of the property, they began slowly making their way back to the entrance in their four-wheel-drive vehicle.

At one of several, almost-hidden crossroads on the trail, they met a man and two teenaged boys. The trio had walked the mile from the entrance road, forded the creek, and was headed towards the waterfalls. One of the teens came to Ken Hay's side of the vehicle and asked him why they were looking at the property. Ken said they were interested in building a Christian camp. The teen brightened and said, "That's exactly what Mr. Moore wants to do. We're looking at the property for him!" Ken gave his phone number to the young man and asked if he would kindly give the information to Mr. Moore since they were interested in the same use for the property. The timing of this "chance" meeting is beyond amazing. It was a God-appointed rendezvous. Only later did it cross the mind of the men that God used a providential meeting with a teenager to help bring about a place where the lives of teenagers would be changed.

On Monday, the realtor called Ken Hay with the news that the Toxaway property was no longer for sale. Mr. Moore had placed money down on the property, effectively taking it off of the market. It was to be another man's dream fulfilled on this beautiful property. Ken's heart sank. His group was back to square one after believing that this property was, indeed, God's will for a new camp.

On Thursday, Ray Moore, the man who now possessed the option on the property, called Ken Hay and asked for a meeting. After the men exchanged explanations of the burden they had for Christian camping, Ray was amazed at the scope of the plans from this unknown group. He was a born-again Christian, and he decided to back away from the option to buy the property.

A complicated situation involving the realtors who had a potential commission in the sale of the property ensued. But ultimately Mr. Dinkins, the original owner of the property, and his family gave an even better price on the ruggedly beautiful tract of land. Through this gracious act, God opened the pathway for the property to be purchased by the newly formed group. On December 19, 1967, the men closed on the property that would later become known as THE WILDS.

One attorney helped the group apply for a state charter, while another assisted in the application process for a new 501(c)(3) missionary organization. Needing a name for the corporation for the purpose of filing papers, the group was incorporated as the Hemlock Hills Christian Association, Inc. because of the abundance of hemlock trees on the property. (In 1987 the corporate name was changed from Hemlock Hills Christian Association to THE WILDS Christian Association, Inc.) Now a new corporation existed; there were board appointments; there was the loan arranged for an astounding $1,000,000; and the work was just beginning.

However, no one should forget the providential meeting in the woods that would change the direction of the lives of thousands of people.

A NAME FOR THE AGES—THE WILDS!

Bob Kembel, a friend of the new ministry was preparing the layout for the first general brochure for the new ministry. Bob's creative juices were at work as he gave several suggestions for a name for the new camp. Hemlock Hills had a certain *lack* of appeal! An ancient philosopher had committed suicide drinking a concoction of juice from the hemlock. Ken Hay remembers one of the suggestions was the Four Seasons Camp and Conference Center; that was eliminated. One name suggested was THE WILDS. The group laughed at first. That name sounded like a newly created rock music group. However, the more they thought about it, the more appealing the name became.

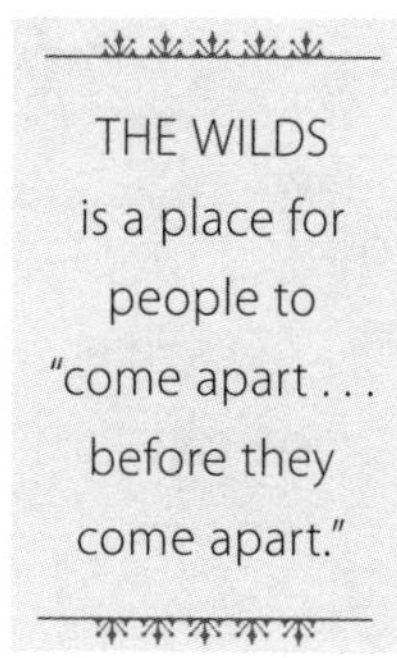
THE WILDS
is a place for
people to
"come apart . . .
before they
come apart."

Jesus had taken His disciples apart to a "wilderness place" to rest, refresh, and pray. Wasn't that one of the reasons why people come to a camp, to come to an out-of-the-way place? Finally it was settled. The new camp was to become known as THE WILDS. It is hard to imagine its being called anything else. Even now, THE WILDS is a place for people to "come apart . . . before they come apart."

Eight hundred and fifteen acres waited to be fashioned into a camp like no other.

In Their Own WORDS

I had my first contact with THE WILDS in early 1969, before any construction took place. My dad and I would wade across the creek and camp out beyond the creek. With axes and saws, we started clearing the road that leads to the falls as we hiked.

Through the years I have come to many of the camps that have been offered. I appreciate the consistency of the staff, because they have provided some of the most consistent Christian living that I have ever witnessed. The outstanding preaching and the dedicated staff make THE WILDS a truly unique organization where everything is done to the glory of God.

—Friend and former camper

Ken Hay—
35-year-old visionary

Diane Hay

Walt Fremont—
ten years of prayer

Carl Blyth

Carl Blyth, Joe Henson, and Ken Hay—the founders

Groundbreaking—Board members Carl Blyth, Joe Henson, Walt Rumminger, Walt Handford, and Walt Fremont

First entrance sign

Groundbreaking 1968—a seed is planted

Present entrance sign

Groundbreaking—
Grace Henson and Diane Hay

Herb and Pearl Mueller—
beloved pioneers

Bob and Ann Stoner—volunteers
turned full-time staff members

Rich Callahan saw the first
fruits of ministry

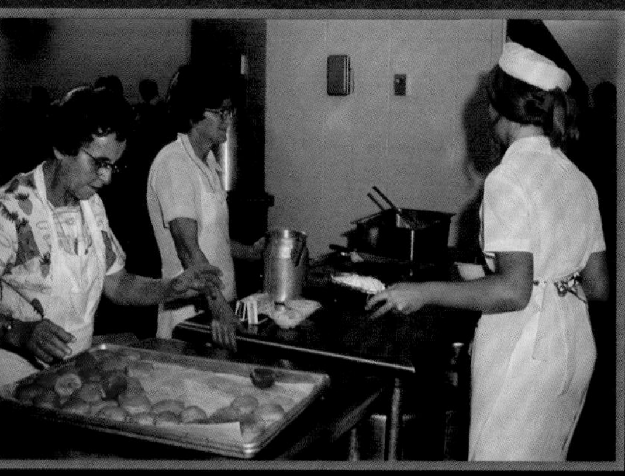
Mrs. Mueller and Mrs. G
(Genovesi, Mardi Collier's
mother) manage the
three crises a day

Marsha Farr VanSteenburg—
first office manager

The balcony—
dirt + sand = showers of blessing

Jerry Sprout—first
field rep, program
director, cleanup
crew chief, and etc.

August 4–10, 1969—
first summer campers

Summer 2007—more than 700
happy campers each week

Bigball—the longest-running game at THE WILDS

Modern Bigball—same as early Bigball

Bigball Bowling—one of many supersized games

The 4th Falls or Great Falls, as it is called locally

The Superslide began as the Mudslide

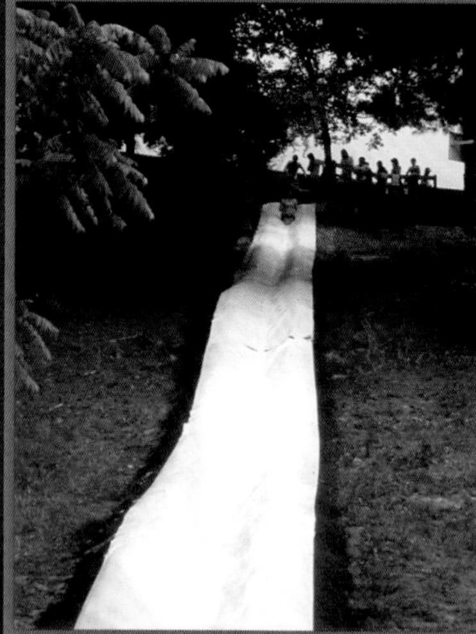

Superslide—the next generation

Tubing styles change, but the object never does!

Tubing—thrills and chills

Water cannons—beware tubers!

The Lake Trolley

The Land Trolley—a gentle glide through the woods

The Giant Swing in action

The Giant Swing just before the release

Harnessed up for a flight on the Giant Swing

The Tarp had its ups and downs

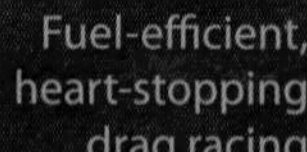

Fuel-efficient, heart-stopping drag racing

The Odysseys hit the trails . . . and other things

Chapter Three

MASTER PLANNING THE MASTER'S PLAN

THIS IS THE LORD'S DOING; IT IS MARVELLOUS IN OUR EYES.

PSALM 118:23

"PUT IT IN WRITING!"

Architect John McCullough from Charlotte, North Carolina, spent a full day at the campsite asking questions to put on paper the thoughts and dreams of both Ken Hay and the vice-president of the ministry, Dr. Joe Henson. The three men were touring the property and getting the feel of the land. What they felt mostly was a cold, penetrating rain that was falling continuously and chilling the three men to the bone.

All-American woodsman Joe set about to get a fire going on the old logging path, wet wood notwithstanding. Mr. McCullough and Ken Hay were huddled in the Jeep endeavoring to stay dry, and John made a suggestion that has become one of the bases for the success of THE WILDS through the years. He recommended to Ken that every idea, dream, and vision should be written down. "Put it in writing" was his mantra.

> To this day, we are never ready to put ideas into practice until we can give biblical reasons in writing for why we do what we do.

This simple, yet profound, practice of putting things in writing became standard practice in all areas of the ministry at THE WILDS. And back in his classroom at Bob Jones University, Ken Hay began requiring his students in his doctrines classes to write down a biblical philosophy of ministry as well, emphasizing right doctrinal understanding. "Put it in writing" for many of these students became the basis of *why they should do what they should do* in life and any future ministry.

Ken, Joe, and Carl spent approximately forty hours brainstorming every idea and putting them into writing. Not many people know that the original dream included a monorail system beginning at Highway 178 and ending in the parking lot at camp. They realized that many details had yet to be considered, and they realized that some ideas, such as a monorail system, would be totally impractical. Yet the principle of "put it in writing" was practiced.

To this day, we are never ready to put ideas into practice until we can give biblical reasons in writing for why we do what we do. A statement made on a dismal, wet, chilly day became the basis for a godly practice that still shapes the ministry of THE WILDS.

THE FOUR PS OF A GOOD CAMP

From the beginning, the ministry of THE WILDS has been based on the "Four Ps of a Good Camp." Even the history will scarcely be understood without them. These four words that start with the letter P build one upon the other and give guidance to everything done at THE WILDS. They give greater understanding to what a good camp is.

#1 A Good Philosophy—The "Why"

Far from being a stuffy word reserved for ancient medieval men who sit around in funny hats arguing the unknowable, **philosophy** gives us the basis of and the reasons for why we do what we do in ministry. Since Christians have the Word of God that stands forever, we go to the words of God in Scripture for our foundation in all things.

The commands and principles contained in God's Word comprise the framework by which THE WILDS operates. Our philosophy, which comes from God's Word, tells us what goals we should be aiming for when a person spends time at THE WILDS. God's Word gives us the reasons for why anything is emphasized and practiced at THE WILDS.

A good camp must have a good philosophy originating from God's eternal Word. There is "none good" but God.

#2 Good People—The "Who"

The biblical philosophy gives guidelines for the kind of **people** who become part of a ministry of THE WILDS. While there are no perfect people and no perfect Christians, it is obvious that only those who are clearly born again through belief and trust in the gospel should be eligible to serve at THE WILDS. Whether it be a member of the board of directors, an administrator, a full-time or seasonal staff member, everyone should be growing in the image and likeness of Christ by interaction with and obedience to the Word of God and thorough saturation in the ministry philosophy.

There have been many talented, personable, wholesome people who have worked at THE WILDS through the years. However, it would be impossible to point campers to a vital, growing relationship with Christ if our people do not know, believe, and follow Christ passionately.

#3 A GOOD PROGRAM—THE "WHAT"

The **program** is the vehicle to show campers how one is able to glorify God and to obey Him in any life situation. The program can be planned by the staff, including activities, hikes, preaching times, devotional times, free times, Funtimes, and mealtimes. But the program can also be the action taken by God alone, including rainy weather, loss of electricity and hot water, times of sickness or injury, and new relationships formed at camp.

Anything and everything that happens at camp—planned or unplanned—is part of the program. Anything and everything allows an alert and sensitive staff member the chance to apply the Truth of God with the love of God to everyday life situations.

The staff uses the total program, planned by man and by God, to teach what it means to "do all to the glory of God."

Refer to chapter eight for a complete listing of the programs that have taken place at THE WILDS.

#4 A GOOD PLACE—THE "WHERE"

The **place** takes last place in order of importance, but it is, nonetheless, very important. Praise the Lord for the beautiful setting and facilities He has provided for THE WILDS.

However, if a good philosophy has brought good people and a good program to a place, a good camp can flourish even if the place is not ideal. In the CampsAbroad ministry, there have been many times when the place camp is held is far from ideal, yet the camp has been tremendously effective because of the good philosophy, people, and program. The place does not have to be new, but it should as clean and in as good repair as possible.

At THE WILDS, there have been wonderful people, an exciting, unique program, and a top-quality place throughout the history. However, hands down, the most important, deciding factor on whether or not THE WILDS is a *good* camp lies in the good philosophy which has us looking to Scripture for that which is good in God's eyes. We have sought to find out what God says is good, and then we have put it in writing.

"WELL, YOU SHOULD'VE BEEN THERE. THE LORD WAS THERE."

The groundbreaking and dedication service for the new property was set for June 1, 1968. Newspaper reporters and even a television reporter were on hand. Government officials and friends from Asheville, Brevard, and Rosman, North Carolina and Greenville, South Carolina were present. In all one hundred twenty-five people made no small effort to be at the ceremony. Each one had to be transported by four-wheel-drive vehicles to ford the creek down by the present girls' cabin area.

The Rosman Rescue Squad had cleared a parking lot on the site of the original caretaker's home (presently the home of Willie and Sarah Partin). A meal was catered from a local Brevard restaurant. Architect John McCullough displayed his concept drawings of the Lodge and the Dining Hall as well as the entire Master Plan which called for four separate camps (a family conference center, a senior high Olympic village, a junior high pioneer village, and a junior-aged Indian village) to be located in various areas on the eight hundred fifteen-acre campsite.

Attending the ceremony was Bob Stoner, an accounting professor at Bob Jones University, along with his wife, Ann. God challenged Bob's heart that day to volunteer to prepare the budgets and keep the books for the fledgling ministry. Ken Hay was grateful, but he could not have known at this time that Bob was to become his indispensable partner in the ministry through the beginning years when finances were always in a critical state. Bob Stoner served voluntarily for many years, and then in June of 1976 he was employed full-time at THE WILDS until his retirement in 2006 after thirty-seven years of service to God at camp.

A number of the original board members were in attendance by the creek side that day, many of whom are still serving as board members or board members emeritus. A great number of their children and grandchildren have been staff members and campers at camp.

A week after the groundbreaking, Ken Hay was meeting with the president of the local electric cooperative and two of his engineers as to the future electrical needs of the new camp. Mr. Sheffield, the president of the cooperative, stopped in midsentence to ask the engineers, "Were you at that groundbreaking last weekend?" Both engineers replied that they had not had the opportunity to be there. Mr. Sheffield intoned, "Well, you should have been, because **the Lord was there**!" He glanced at a stunned Ken Hay and told him that he was a born-again lay preacher, and he was impacted by the Lord at the groundbreaking.

We all know that God is always present with us, but Ken Hay has often reminisced about that day long ago and reiterates that the strong desire of his heart is that every person who visits the campsite will be aware of God's presence in that same personal, lasting, and life-changing way. Regularly the comment is made by campers nearing the campsite, "The closer I get to the gate, the more I sense that I'm coming to a place that is a little bit of heaven on earth."

Like the New Jerusalem, it is true that "The Lord is there!"

In Their Own WORDS

George was the camp missionary speaker for the summers, and Marilyn was in charge of the craft program. We are grateful for the summers of ministry He gave us at THE WILDS. Seeing souls saved and changed and experiencing God's power actively working in teen and adult lives were all special memories we had of those early days. It thrilled our hearts to see young people surrender to the call for missions, and then to see them later serving the Lord in other lands. We have been blessed to see the lives of children, grandchildren, and many friends enriched because of the ministry of THE WILDS.

—George and Marilyn Jensen (1971–1978 staff)

Chapter Four
Rise Up and Build

Then I told them of the hand of my God which was good upon me; as also the king's words that he had spoken unto me. And they said, Let us rise up and build. So they strengthened their hands for this good work.

Nehemiah 2:18

There is no better picture in Scripture to describe those early construction days than the story of Nehemiah. The founders, Ken, Joe, and Carl, virtually lived the story of Nehemiah, the king's cupbearer, who had an immense task ahead of him that could only be accomplished by the power of God.

During the early days of THE WILDS construction, Old Toxaway and Frozen Creek roads became well-nigh impassable because of heavy rains. The gravel roads with their hairpin turns proved all but impossible for the trucks carrying building materials to make it to the new campsite. Especially troublesome were the trucks carrying the beams for the Lodge and Dining Hall. It was necessary in some situations for a crane to follow the trucks. The crane would lift the tail end of the trailer, still attached to the tractor, and swing it around the hairpin curves. Several drivers surveying the stretches of roads they would be navigating simply would not attempt the last five miles. The torrential rains kept the country roads so unstable that at times the construction workers would have to walk the last mile up the steep hill to the campsite worksite each morning. Many quit rather than endure the inconvenience. The challenges were enormous.

Ray Moore was the project manager (yes, the same Ray Moore who gave up his option on the property making it available to us) for the main buildings and the famous summer cabins that came to be known as the birdhouses. There are several outstanding reasons why the name *birdhouse* was the perfect name. They looked like birdhouses, and an argument could be made that they were small enough to *be* birdhouses. Paul Ramsey, a contractor affiliated with Camp Berean in Indiana, designed these famous dwellings. In February of 1969, he came to camp and set up a jig to enable future workers to crank out forty-seven of these "deluxe condos" at a cost of five hundred dollars each, including mattresses. The birdhouses were supposed to be temporary, being used for only a few years. However, they became permanent because funds were greatly necessary for other pressing needs of the camp. The birdhouses were "temporarily" used for twenty-eight years before they were retired with great honor. Three birdhouses remain as a living history of those times.

Presently, in place of these pseudomansions, pleasant and roomy duplex summer cabins are universally appreciated. Of course, anyone who had the birdhouse experience deserves the highest esteem. They just don't make architectural beauties like that anymore! In the eyes of most, the absence of birdhouses was considered a blessing, but in the eyes of many, they are a memory to be treasured for a lifetime!

Work continued throughout the winter and into the spring of 1969 in preparation for the first three weeks of summer camp in the history of THE WILDS. The dam at the eight-acre lake was being constructed using the dirt from the bed of the future lake as well as from the high knoll that was shaved off to provide room for the Lodge. By the beginning of camp the first year, there was insufficient time for the lake to fill. So the camp went on without its use.

> These guys came into a situation that could be described as Spartan.

Around the first of June the very first staff members in the history of THE WILDS arrived. These twenty-five college- and high-school-aged boys had the responsibility of readying the campsite for those initial camps, which were slated to begin the latter part of July. These guys came into a situation that could be described as Spartan. Working electricity was virtually nonexistent. One of the men, Tim Farr, who was studying to enter law school, would go to his car each evening and study his law texts by his dome light. There was no running water. The shower facilities were natural, to say the least. The bathing procedure was to don the bathing suit, take shampoo and a bar of soap to the creek, and bathe as the pioneers did.

Food was cooked on propane gas stoves. Barbara Black and Diane Hay's mother, Pearl Mueller, labored ably as cooks. Plywood sheets on top of sawhorses served as tables and cut-to-order logs served as chairs. These dining accoutrements were not an issue to the men because the food was hearty and delicious. What more could college guys want?

Half of the young men worked at constructing the birdhouses, and the other half were placed under the direction of landscape expert, Herb Mueller, father of Diane Hay and retired railroad man. In his midseventies, "Dad" Mueller could work college men into the ground by simply insisting they stay up with him. One of the boys volunteered for Dad Mueller's crew thinking, *So how hard can following a seventy-five-year-old man down some mountain roads be?* He found out! That "old man" could work circles around the young guys, and he left them totally exhausted. Dad Mueller continued to mow the steep and expansive hill between the Lodge and Ballfield even when he was in his early eighties. The entrance sign is dedicated to the memory of those pioneers, Herb and Pearl Mueller, who left such an example and made such an impact in those beginning days.

For the thousands who have made their way to one of the beautiful waterfalls at THE WILDS campsite, did you ever wonder who "planned" those challenging trails? Part of the first landscape crew's responsibility was to experiment and find the trails from the primitive road down to the waterfalls in anticipation of those first campers' arrival. Up and down the mountain they would tread day after day, having run-ins with unfriendly snakes and bees. The process was to mark the possible routes, tracing and retracing their steps until an acceptable route could be found. Many campers contend they did a poor job, making the mountains too high and the trails too steep.

As a reward for the hard work of both the landscape and construction crews, the day would occasionally end at the big rock at the 4th Falls. One of the staff workers, Tom Hitchcock, would sing in a rich baritone voice *How Great Thou Art*. The boys would all join on the chorus with that beautiful creation of God providing the accompaniment. None of these men, and few other people, had ever experienced a created masterpiece like this one hundred twenty-five foot waterfall right in their own backyard.

Those reflective moments were becoming fewer and farther between. The opening of camp was only a couple of weeks away, but much work remained. It was time for reinforcements before the last push to the first camp in the history of THE WILDS.

In Their Own WORDS

The facilities and environment are a terrific setting for the learning that occurs throughout the camp week. It is reassuring to know that THE WILDS reinforces the same teaching that the teens receive at home in our churches for fifty-one weeks out of the year. I am assured that when we travel to THE WILDS, our teens, my wife, and I will never return home the same.

—Youth pastor

I remember hiking to a huge waterfall. It was a very long and hard hike, but it was really beautiful. I hope that campers are still enjoying it as much I did.

—Former camper

Chapter Five

THE FIRST WEEK OF CAMP

THE LORD HATH DONE GREAT THINGS
FOR US; WHEREOF WE ARE GLAD.

PSALM 126:3

For the twenty-five male staff members, the arrival of the female staff members towards the last week of July in 1969 was memorable. They benefited from the softening effects the girls had on everything from conversations to point of view. Although much had been done in preparation for the campers' arrival on August 4, there was still much to be done. Cabins had to be arranged and cleaned. Dining Hall tables and chairs had to be removed from shipping boxes and set up. Furniture had to be placed in the Lodge rooms, painting had to be completed, and the clutter of nonstop construction had to be cleaned up.

The campgrounds themselves needed much attention. There was a massive twelve- to fourteen-foot high pile of limbs, tree stumps, and brush in the main parking lot of the Lodge. From experience everyone knew that, besides being an eyesore, the piles of brush brought unwanted visitors in the form of snakes and bees.

The whole campsite was a maze of open ditches crisscrossing the parking lot, down the hill behind the Snack Shop, and onto the Ballfield. Adding to the picture, torrential rains fell. Stands of grass had not yet taken hold, so the whole camp was a quagmire with ankle-deep mud in some places.

To the boys, all of these things were normal. To the girls, one had to wonder if they were shocked and alarmed at the sight! But they were resilient, and there were no complaints from this crew of pioneer ladies.

Staff Training Week

Staff Training Week, the critical week of training before campers come in for the season, became something much different. It became Camp Preparation Week. Throughout the day the staff cleaned, hauled, and put together furniture. In the evenings after dinner, Ken Hay—with the help of staff members Joe and Grace Henson, Frank and Flora Jean Garlock, Carl and Carol Blyth, Jerry Sprout, and Marsha Farr Van Steenburgh—readied the young staff with training in counseling and new procedures. Like all Staff Training Weeks at THE WILDS, it was a week of bonding the hearts together for the ministry ahead. The few short days of training flew by, and finally it was time for the arrival of the most important ingredient at camp—the campers!

"Finally, They're Here!"

One hundred and fifty enthusiastic teenagers, paying only twenty-five dollars for the entire week, swept into the camp on that first day.

There were new buildings (mostly finished), a new campsite, a new program, new procedures, and a brand-new staff. There were also new experiences for the campers since the electricity was more off than on, meaning the water pumps could not function and insuring that the showers would not work. The girls had the delight of washing their hair in the cool mountain stream just like they had seen in television commercials. Some were so taken with the experience that they continued it even when the water was functioning. The boys soon fell into the pattern of soap, towel, and swimming trunks at bathing time.

Before the first service was held, a teenager had come to Christ, not even with the help of his counselor, but with a crew member who cared.

Registration had barely begun on that first day, when the Snack Shop opened for the very first time in camp history. Rich Callahan, a cleanup crew member for the first week (staff members alternated between counselor and operational staff positions in the first years) was standing beside a camper from Columbia, South Carolina. Making conversation as they waited for a snack, Rich asked the boy if he had ever been saved. The young man answered, "No, I've never done that." Rich asked him if he would like to be born again, and the young man enthusiastically said, "Yes, I would!" Before the program began, and even before the first service was held, a teenager had come to Christ, not even with the help of his counselor, but with a crew member who cared. This was a wonderful commencement to the ministry of the newborn camp called THE WILDS. This young man was the firstfruit of the thousands who have since come to Christ on the campsite.

The pressure was on the kitchen during that premier week. Already the kitchen handled the proverbial "three crises a day"—breakfast, lunch, and dinner. Now add to that stew the fact that the electricity was wholly erratic. It clicked from on to off seemingly on a whim. Diane Hay, Pearl Mueller, Barbara Black, and others knew that cooking for sixteen boys over a small gas burner was not in the same league with cooking for two hundred hungry first-time campers and staff in an all-electric kitchen with an unreliable power source. In the midst of talking food companies into coming to the ends of the world to deliver products and hefting number ten cans (cans are no longer referred to by number, but are now referred to by weight) of vegetables and pudding to the storage shelves, the willing lady soldiers in the kitchen had to always be thinking, "What is Plan B if we cannot cook and heat the food?" The invention of bread, peanut butter, and jelly never seemed so grand. The Lord's hand was on the switch throughout the week. The power outages occurred, but never at a time to sabotage the meals. The campers were oblivious to the pressure, and, as typical at THE WILDS, they were always satisfied with the good food.

On the first night, program men Jerry Sprout, Nicky Chavers, and, of course, Ken Hay wheeled out the six-foot cage ball. It was the first one most campers had ever seen. This game, with very little interruption, has been played every week of every summer for the entire history of THE WILDS. In the early days, because of the small crowds, the boys and girls played the game together. Like a kickoff at a football game, both teams would start about twenty yards from the Bigball. When the whistle blew, the race was on and the collision was imminent. What a train wreck it was! There were always a couple of boys who were fast enough to get to the ball ahead of the others. That was not necessarily good for them. They would hit the ball right before the main body of charging campers got there. When that happened, the recoil sent the early arrivals sprawling into their teammates, clearing out the first line of players. It is no wonder that the rules of the game have changed to favor the health and safety of campers . . . but it was fun!

The Centipede Relay was one of the games everyone anticipated that first week. In true centipede fashion, every team member grabbed onto a long rope. The two teams lined up side by side, the whistle blew, and only the team captain knew where the course was taking them. Across the Ballfield and around the light pole was only the beginning. Already the faster team members were learning to wait and gage their speed to accommodate slower teammates. Everyone had to maintain their hold on the rope for the giant centipede to legally travel. Over the log bridge and back through the creek the race went. Running all the way from the Ballfield to the Lake (a grueling race even for a person in shape), the race continued. Out into the shallow part of the Lake and around a rowboat the very tired, many-legged creature sloshed, the taller, bigger campers supporting the smaller ones through the water. The finish line was on the Ballfield, and the crowning obstacle thought up by the program staff was yet to come. Running behind the Snack Shop, the centipede jumped into one of the open ditches leading from the top to the bottom of the hill. These yawning ditches were to be used to bury cables which were yet to be laid. Did anyone know the ditch, which was three feet deep and a foot and a half wide, was also home to mud at least four to six inches deep? The tired but game giant critters plunged ahead as one after another pair of feet became shoeless, the mud literally sucking the shoes from the feet. There was no time to stop to retrieve them, of course. There was a game to be won! Give everything—including shoes and socks—for the team! The cleanup crew spent the next day shoveling buried shoes from the ditches, but it was memorable! (The anguished scream of mothers may have been heard across the land the following Saturday night when campers arrived back home.)

There was a game to be won! Give everything—including shoes and socks—for the team!

At the close of the Thursday night service, Ken Hay stood before the group and tried to apologize for the rain, the mud, the lack of electricity, and the absence of water, not from the sky, but from the pipes. He complimented them on being great pioneers in what he hoped would become one of the best camps in America. Almost as if on cue, every camper rose to his feet and gave an ovation that lasted some seven minutes. One of the counselors, Paul Bixby, spontaneously started THE WILDS theme song:

> *W* stands for wonderful.
> *I* means it's ideal.
> *L* stands for loving Christ and living life in Him.
> *D* is for doing right.
> *S* we're saved to serve.
> *W–I–L–D–S* spells WILDS, WILDS, WILDS!

Ken Hay stood weeping, and staff members realized they had experienced something so unusual and remarkable that they would likely remember it through their entire lifetime. THE WILDS was at last doing what it was called to do!

After the campers had pulled out and the mud had settled for the weekend, Frank Garlock, the camp music director, wrote another rendition of THE WILDS theme song, much to the delight and enjoyment of the staff. Sung to the same tune he wrote:

> *W* stands for wilderness.
> *I* means I got lost.
> *L* stands for leaking pipes and lights that will not work.
> *D* is for droopy drawers.
> *S* for snakes and sand.
> *W–I–L–D–S* spells work, work, work!

In Their Own WORDS

We have enjoyed so many great times at THE WILDS throughout the years. I was a junior camper at the first junior camp in 1969. How well I remember the good time I had that summer. None of us wanted to go home. I attended the first CIT program that was offered. I have attended as a youth director and now as a senior pastor. We certainly praise the Lord for the ministry of THE WILDS.

—Former camper, now senior pastor

Section Two

SKIPPING ACROSS THE MOUNTAINS

Ken Hay has always stated that he believes "it is harder to keep something going than it is to start it." For ones who study the history of THE WILDS, it is difficult to imagine that being true. He may be the only human who can judge this. However, through the first four decades of THE WILDS, there have been people, messages, incidents, events, innovative concepts, and maxims too numerous to mention which have shaped the path of this ministry. Touching a few of these highlights can be likened to skipping across these beautiful mountains, pausing only briefly to touch some of the peaks and to occasionally explore a valley or two. Whether these facts are old or new to you, they became part of the history of THE WILDS, and they help us understand why the ministry of THE WILDS is the way it is today. Let us touch a few of the peaks and valleys together.

Chapter Six

Those Happy, Wholesome Weekends

AND JESUS, WHEN HE CAME OUT, SAW MUCH PEOPLE,
AND WAS MOVED WITH COMPASSION TOWARD THEM,
BECAUSE THEY WERE AS SHEEP NOT HAVING A SHEPHERD:
AND HE BEGAN TO TEACH THEM MANY THINGS.

MARK 6:34

In 1969, the Vietnam War was at its peak. The hippie movement was in its heyday. Civil rights rallies and protests were daily news. Rock music had experienced yet another metamorphosis for the worse. Outright rejection of national and parental authorities was rampant. Teenagers were becoming a force and were influencing fashion and financial markets. And churches were looking for partners to help in the struggle to reach the hearts of the youth of America.

The leadership of THE WILDS knew that the summertime was the obvious season full to overflowing with opportunities. But they were not totally sure what part the fledgling ministry could play in the nonsummer months. Very little had been done through the years with year-round camping. It was the goal of the leadership to host at least five weekend retreats, yet it was not clear how retreats could be advertised or how they would be received.

The students wanted to pray. They wanted to obey. During that time of cynicism, this was an unheard-of response and was even chronicled in the local newspaper.

There was still a flickering openness to Christianity in the public schools of the country. A great number of teachers in public schools were Christians with an unapologetic testimony for Christ, and the government had not yet interjected itself forcefully into the public school scene. Several Christian teachers saw a golden opportunity in the willingness of teenagers to try anything adventurous. Russ McCall, the soccer coach at Parker High School in Greenville, South Carolina, recruited his players, along with players from the school football team and cheerleading squads, to come to THE WILDS immediately following a fall football game. Before the weekend was over, some forty-four students professed faith in Christ.

Another teacher, Andy Anderson, a teacher at Hillcrest High School in the Greenville area, recruited one hundred students for a weekend retreat. Many of these students trusted Christ as Savior. The Monday after the retreat, the teachers at the high school were in for an extreme shock. Typically the students were hesitant to salute the flag and say the Pledge of Allegiance. On that Monday, there were complaints that not every room had an accessible flag of the United States. The students wanted to pray. They wanted to obey. During that time of cynicism, this was an unheard-of response and was even chronicled in the local newspaper. The obedience of the student body to instructions rose so obviously, that more and more young people wanted to know, "What is happening at our school?" Witnessing opportunities abounded.

At Northwood Middle School, teacher Leon Peninger was able to bring one hundred twenty students to THE WILDS. That weekend, sixty-seven of the students placed their trust in Christ. One counselor at the retreat gave the following testimony: "I had never experienced anything like it my life! I had ten high school boys from the public schools in my cabin (a converted Lodge room in the East Wing) for the weekend. They were excited about everything. They played Bigball with reckless abandon. They were tubing the creek in forty-degree weather. They were jumping into the frigid 4th Falls with no hesitation. But what amazed me was the rapt attention they gave during the messages. Major Ron Brooks shared his stories of being a helicopter pilot in the Vietnam Conflict. He told of his youthful, capable copilot, Sandy, who had no time for God in his life and how he was suddenly taken into eternity during a mission. Major Brooks got to the good news of the gospel, and I could tell their hearts were tender. They were deeply convicted about the fact that their sins were unwashed. After chapel the next morning, I gave instructions for them to follow during the God & I Time. We were all on the hillside below the Lodge about ten yards apart. It was a beautiful sight to see those worldly guys peering into John 3 and the words of eternal life. I began to approach each one and asked them if they would like to trust Christ today. Though they had differing personalities, each one looked me in the eyes and said, 'Yes, I want to be saved.' Eight guys trusted Christ on that hillside within the space of an hour. It is any wonder that these are among my most treasured memories at THE WILDS?"

The most extreme recruiting for weekend retreats may have been done by a young pastor/businessman by the name of Bob Wood. He was the founding pastor of Killian Hill Baptist Church in Lilburn, Georgia, and would later become the executive vice-president of Bob Jones University. During his ministry in the Atlanta area, he would drive buses to the various high school football games or to the notorious hippie hangouts on 14th Street in Atlanta. He would advertise that there would be a weekend in the mountains for teens. Teens would hop on the bus having no clue where it would end up, but perfectly willing for an adventure. Many came to Christ.

It is evident that times have changed. That offer could not be extended or accepted in this day and time, but it caused THE WILDS to literally burst on the scene in the effort to help churches in their outreach to teens. Can you imagine the excitement as the college-aged counselors came back to their dorm rooms after the retreat was over and enthusiastically recounted the miracles of the weekend?

Those first retreats were not only fast paced for the campers, but they were even more intense for the staff. There were no staff members living on the campsite during the week, carefully planning each detail and waiting expectantly for campers to arrive. The staff struggled to make it up the mountain before the campers themselves arrived! Such was the case for the only full-time staff members of THE WILDS at the time, all of whom worked out of THE WILDS office in the basement of Ken and Diane Hay's home. The first secretary of the camp, Marsha Farr Van Steenburgh, had to do all of the office work, recruit staff, arrange for the logistics and transportation, and then race to camp to do cleanup and registration. Diane Hay, a full-time professor of home economics at Bob Jones University would have to finish her teaching day, pack the groceries she had purchased all over town for the retreat menu (no food company would deliver small quantities), pick her children up from school, and make it up to camp in time to set up the Dining Hall and prepare the food. For Ken Hay, the whirlwind of activity was much the same. He would pack the family, pack the supplies, and pack the Bible and sermon notes, because he was usually the main speaker and program voice. For Jerry Sprout, the first Field Representative/Program Director/Cleanup Crew Chief/ Newsletter Editor/Transportation Chief, the frantic schedule was routine. Nearly every weekend, Tom and Marilyn Hill became the Cleanup Crew Chief and Dining Room Hostess respectively after a week of teaching and staff responsibilities at Bob Jones University. All of the Hay and Hill children would contribute to the hard work, even if they had to stand on crates and stepladders to accomplish the tasks. Each family and individual would do his part in the cleanup on Sunday, make it to church on Sunday evening, and show up for another week of ministry responsibilities on Monday morning. A pioneer ministry requires much sacrifice.

A pioneer ministry requires much sacrifice.

During those first few years of retreats, the registration for camp was generally last minute, so it was rare to know exact numbers of campers attending. Since there were no winterized cabins and no Dorm, the staff had to deploy into the North and East Wings of the Lodge and prepare the rooms by taking down all of the motel furniture and putting up the bunk beds, affectionately called "knuckle busters." The massive metal beds were no respecters of persons doing damage to toes, shins, fingers, and knuckles of directors and counselors alike. After placing as many of the menacing beds in the motel rooms as possible, there were often more beds needed. Extra unregistered campers would always show up to enjoy the excitement of the weekend. So rooms were retrofitted with additional mattresses to go in the closets and halls. Occasionally, a camper would volunteer to sleep in the bathtub, which was ultradangerous with mischievous pranksters everywhere. A turn of the faucet on the unsuspecting sleeper was tempting—in many cases *too* tempting. After the weekend was over and the camp was clean, loyal helpers took down those sinister bunk beds and dutifully replaced the beds with the original motel furniture amid the ubiquitous cries of pain and aggravation. The knuckle busters always got their man. They now reside in the Dormitory, having been welded together, seldom moved, and no longer despised.

The goal to have five weekend retreats in the initial season after the opening of THE WILDS was far surpassed. As it turned out, there were barely five weekends which did *not* contain some type of program. Weekend retreats continue to energize both young people and adults at camp. From the supercharged but comparatively small beginning, the nonsummer seasons have grown to the point where there are over ten thousand people attending retreats from September through May.

In Their Own WORDS

It was a happy day for me today as I helped my daughter pack for her first week at THE WILDS. As I did this, I was reminiscing about my first experience as a cook in 1969. Working there as "a pioneer" was a joy and a thrill, but now I see the same place through different eyes. Nineteen years later I am sending my own precious daughter there, along with my prayers that the Lord will speak and work in her heart and life. This is a camp I can trust and feel one hundred percent confident that my daughter will come home a stronger Christian as she allows God to work in her life.

—Former cook, now mother

Barbara and I had the privilege of surveying the property that is now THE WILDS with Carl Blyth in his Jeep before the land was purchased. It was clear that this would be a special place. It has been a joy to see the property go from nothing, to birdhouses, and now to the facilities God has raised up today. To God be the glory!

Two special memories come to mind as I think about the early days. I remember the public school weekend retreats and the scores of kids who received Christ as Savior. What a blessing! Of course, the most vivid memory for me would be the Army-Navy weeks during the summer. The competition was fierce, but the preaching of the Word of God and the faithfulness of a dedicated counseling staff turned everything to the glory of God. Praise God for Coach "Rock" Royer (and later Coach John Cartwright) with the Navy teams, and I thank God for the time I had with the Army teams. Touch football may have been the sports competition, but we all worked together for the souls of those teens. Yes, those are good memories. To God be the glory!

—Major Ron Brooks

Chapter Seven

Activities—Good, Clean Fun!

THEN WAS OUR MOUTH FILLED WITH LAUGHTER,
AND OUR TONGUE WITH SINGING:
THEN SAID THEY AMONG THE HEATHEN, THE LORD
HATH DONE GREAT THINGS FOR THEM.

PSALM 126:2

Adults and children love THE WILDS because there are so many out of the ordinary things to do. One of the publications of the camp, the *S.O.A.P.* publication, is named with an acrostic that gives the reasons for having unique activities at camp. *S.O.A.P.* contains all these elements of good, clean fun:

S: Surprise
O: Originality
A: Adventure
P: Purpose

Each one of the truly classic activities and events are filled with the elements of good, clean fun, and if you have ever been at THE WILDS, the memories of these will bring a smile and maybe a shiver or two!

BIGBALL

Also called cage ball, these colorful balls covered with canvas or nylon and housing a rubberized bladder pumped full of air are a symbol of all that is unique and fun about THE WILDS. From day one, the Bigball game has been a must-do for every camper who comes to THE WILDS. Whether you loved it or feared it, whether you came out bruised or unscathed, whether you ended up at the bottom of the pile anxious for your life or you got that big hit that brought the winning score, whether you "just got to touch it" or were one of the stalwarts for your team, Bigball was the event that announced to everyone, "Camp has begun. I'm at THE WILDS, and my team is going to beat your team!"

The Bigball at THE WILDS comes in all sizes: three-foot, four-foot, five-foot, and even six-foot. It has been the creative centerpiece for such games as Bigball Foosball, Bigball Croquet, Bigball Basketball, Bigball Baseball, Bigball Soccer, Bigball Tetherball, and even Bigball Bowling. It is hard to imagine life without these giant friends around.

THE 4TH FALLS

A hike to the 4th Falls has always been a rite of passage at the camp. Everyone says, "You've just got to see the 4th Falls. It's the granddaddy of them all!" "It's so beautiful!" "That was the most refreshing swim I've ever had!" "Oh, wow, this is the most amazing sight I've ever seen!"

Or maybe your comments and opinions ran in a slightly different mode such as, "How far is it back to camp?" "I can't believe you made us do this!" "I've got to climb up that?" "I'm staying here; I can't go another step." "There are ropes up the hill! I've got to climb up ropes?" "Where's the bathroom?" "Where's the water fountain?" "I promise, if I ever get out of this alive . . ."

All of these statements and many more are stated about the most beautiful part of THE WILDS, the part that our Creator God made with His own words and hands. Nothing matches the beauty of what God has done. The 4th Falls at THE WILDS and its three other companion waterfalls are simply God's masterpieces.

The Superslide

It was a cold camp week where the sun refused to shine. Every game that could be played inside and out had been played to the point of exhaustion. It was the mid 1970s, and the rain had been falling since the campers arrived. The Activity Center did not yet exist, and there was no covered area where three hundred people could play inside and stay dry. The Snack Shop was brimming with teen campers, but one can only play so much Ping-Pong. Program man George Thornton said, "I'm going to do it!"

The "it" he referred to was something that had been talked about, but had never been done—sliding down the steep hill behind the Snack Shop. His goal was to capture the attention and participation of campers whose spirits were flagging. He launched himself over the hill and slid ten to twelve feet. Back up the hill George went to try again. This time he made it twenty feet. Dave Cleary, the resident daredevil, hit the hill flying, outdistancing George's first two efforts. Then a camper asked, "Can I try that?" He did, and one of the oldest, most unique activities at THE WILDS was born!

The unsightliness of the muddy scar on the hillside behind the Snack Shop made the event move to the less noticeable side of the hill behind the North Wing of the Lodge. But after a few rides, rocks and roots were getting unearthed, and jeans and bodies were getting the tougher end of the deal! Along came an enterprising soul who wondered if black poly plastic would make things smoother and faster. It did. Farther and faster the slide went.

> The 4th Falls at THE WILDS and its three other companion waterfalls are simply God's masterpieces.

Through the years it changed. "Hey, what if we dug a trench so we could stay on the plastic and more in the groove?" Another few months passed. "Hey, isn't there some kind of heavy rubberized material—some kind of heavy tarp—that won't rip when we slide on it? Yeah, that's better!" Ron Ellison, then our resident summer staff engineer, suggested we add asphalt and a platform and make the ride take you right into the creek! Wow! That was fast—and what a refreshing shock at the end!

Finally the suggestion was made to build a pool at the bottom for a slow-me-down entry and to make sure the ones at the top knew better when the next one could slide. Through the years the Superslide has changed in detail, but not in purpose. Some call it rugged. Some call it homely. A few have gone for the record number of slides in one afternoon (seventy-plus)! Everyone knows that the Superslide is one of the oldest and most popular friends of campers at THE WILDS.

TUBING IN THE TOXAWAY CREEK

How simple? What fun! Thousands of campers have made dozens, if not hundreds, of trips down the creek in a tube. The announcement during the camper orientation goes something like this: "Simply grab a tube off the tube rack and plop yourself in the creek by the Superslide. Be careful to stop where the sign says, 'Tubing stops here!' because a trip over the waterfalls can change your personality!"

Since the earliest days of the camp, when those heavy, black, truck-tire inner tubes were the only way to float, tubing has consistently been one of the most natural and popular activities for young and old. This is one of the reasons you come to the mountains and one of the fun things about coming to THE WILDS. Is it a rainy day? All the better! Do you remember those early morning and midafternoon tubing adventures in the creek? Nowadays you may want to get out before you tangle with the mischievous guys and girls manning the water cannons at the end of the ride! Tubing is still the greatest!

The Lake Trolley

A Ron Ellison and Rick Jensen production, the Lake Trolley has been around for thirty-six years, beginning with a tower on the island which ran towards the main road. Later it was moved to its present station amid all of the other activities at the Lake.

No one had to tell you to "hang on tight!" You were extremely motivated to not let go—until the second time! Several generations now have looked forward to the zip and the splash from this classic display of good, clean fun.

The Land Trolley

In 1985 an exciting new activity was born. What the program called for was a zip line that one could hold onto and glide across the creek. What was hatched up in the minds of Rick Jensen and Ron Ellison, with help from Neil Cushman, Bill Ertel, and Dan Brooks, was a four hundred twenty-five foot trolley ride from one mountain to another.

Do you remember your first time being hooked up to the pulley mechanism? Could you trust the harness? Could you trust the cable? Did you trust that the "good-lookin' " program guy knew what he was doing when he fastened you in? Could you get over the jitters?

Could you take the ribbing and catcalls from your "friends" way, way down there in the landing area? Would you succumb to peer pressure? "Oh well, here we go!" And there you went.

It has been a quarter of a century and more for this most relaxing ride of all for campers of all ages!

THE GIANT SWING

It was supposed to look and act like an ordinary swing set, only higher and bigger. What it ended up being was something indescribable for a camp. Rick Jensen, with the knowledgeable help and consultation assistance from a volunteer engineer, developed the Giant Swing in 1995. It is an activity that may cause you to pinch yourself to believe that it really exists at THE WILDS—and then you may have kicked yourself for actually trying it.

The Giant Swing is a signature event at camp. Sixty-five feet to the top it goes, and the automatic release triggers all kinds of reactions—screaming, yelling, praying, and even total, stunned silence! Whether campers go down the Giant Swing every time they come to camp or just one time to "prove something" or zero times ("I'll just watch, thank you!"), this is one of the innovative activities that makes THE WILDS unique.

Tim Artus, the Marine and former graphic design artist at THE WILDS, had the privilege of being the first solo "astronut" to ride the contraption. Rick Jensen, the designer, and his daughter Leticia had the honor being the first twosome to swing on the Giant Swing.

How do you top this? Only time will tell.

People come to THE WILDS to have good, clean fun, and through the years, no one has had to go away disappointed. Fun is part of the refreshing enjoyment of life in Christ at a place called THE WILDS!

In Their Own WORDS

I want to tell whoever is reading this that I had so-o-o-o much fun at camp this summer. The games were fun and I met some really nice friends. I came to camp thinking that I was not going to make any decision for Christ because I was on "vacation"! Once I got there, the Lord started speaking to my heart, and I realized that I was not saved. The last night I got saved, and I can already see the difference in my life. I still have a lot of changing to do, but with the Lord's help, I want to keep growing and changing.

—*Camper*

Chapter Eight

All-Star Programs

If any man speak, let him speak as the oracles of God; if any man minister, let him do it as of the ability which God giveth:that God in all things may be glorified through Jesus Christ,to whom be praise and dominion for ever and ever. Amen.

1 Peter 4:11

Christian camping at THE WILDS is limited only by the imagination. No matter how campers can be placed together—by age, station in life, interest, and relationships—there can be another program created to strengthen an area of spiritual need. In the history of THE WILDS there have been over thirty different programs, and new programs are added as the needs arise. The joke at one time was to get so specific as to develop a camp to teach "left-handed juniors boys how to throw rocks!" Only afterwards was it realized that left-handed juniors do that naturally.

There have been camps for men, ladies, teens, juniors, families, businessmen, father and sons, mothers and daughters, college and career, deacons, preachers, married couples, engaged couples, soccer teams, volleyball teams, seminary students, Christian counselors, and the list goes on and on.

Here are a few of the programs that can be deemed All-Stars for the continually blessed ministries they have provided. Many of the readers of this book have doubtless participated in one or more of these special programs. These have to be considered the trademark of THE WILDS and its All-Star programs because of their impact and longevity.

Summer Teen Camps

This one must be mentioned first. The summer teen camps are the flagship of THE WILDS. Starting from the beginning with a summer crowd of one hundred fifty teens, the summers now fill as many as ten weeks of camp with a median number of seven hundred fifty teens each week. There is room for very little else in the summer months.

The name THE WILDS has over the years become synonymous with teenagers; over a half a million young people have come to summer camp at THE WILDS. God has revolutionized and changed thousands of these young people for His glory at summer camp. For many youth groups, this is the highlight of summer. For many young people, this proves to be the highlight of their lives!

Staff Training Week

For forty-plus years, a summer staff consisting of college-aged leaders and future leaders of families have come to THE WILDS as members of the summer staff. Staff members learn the fundamentals of "how to counsel" as well as take part in a Personal Discipleship and Accountability program (PDA) throughout the summer. Each staff member sits down with his supervisor on two occasions during the summer to discuss goals and progress made during the season.

The opportunity to teach these young adults the next step in ministry and the next skill in the Christian life is among the greatest privileges the full-time staff of THE WILDS enjoys—a gift from God. Who would not want to disciple two hundred fifty eager Christian leaders for almost three months of time?

Once a staff member serves in the summer, he is a family member of THE WILDS from that time on.

Once a staff member serves in the summer, he is a family member of THE WILDS from that time on, and the lessons learned become a part of the fabric of his life.

Summer Sponsor Program

Each summer approximately twelve hundred sponsors attend summer camp along with their teens and juniors. They do more than just drop the kids off and hang around all week. Sponsors attend a camp for themselves embedded into the Teen and Junior Camp. Included in their weekly schedule are prayer meetings, informal conferences, as well as youth-work training and philosophy sessions. They can enjoy an optional round of golf, softball with the staff, sand volleyball tournaments, a white-water rafting adventure, and much more.

The staff also encourages the sponsors to be involved in the lives of their teens and juniors during the week by attending their services and activities. They are encouraged to join in the campers' play at free time and to join them on scheduled hikes. The impact of this program has been great.

One former sponsor, Dick Reid, has served for many years as the Director of Development and is currently the vice-president of THE WILDS Christian Association. The former bank president recognized a call to God's work while serving as a sponsor at camp.

Junior Boot Camp (JBC)

Like its bigger brother, Teen Camp, Junior Boot Camp for campers age nine through twelve has been around from the very beginning in 1969. Until 2001 camp for juniors took place during two of the ten weeks of the summer camping program. However, the dreams of the founders had always been to have a junior outpost camp running concurrently with a full complement of teen programs.

An informal master plan for a junior camp was drawn up, but the costs were staggering. From the creative mind of former Program Director Rand Hummel (presently the director of TWNE) came a proposal to minimize the huge cost of a brand-new campsite that duplicated all the services of the main camp. The result is a bustling, energy-infused campsite just moments away from the main campsite.

Junior Boot Camp has its own General Headquarters (the Lakeside Center), its own Drill Hall, its own lighted Ballfield, and its own activity areas. Junior Boot Camp is busy making godly, youthful memories for up to two hundred twenty-five juniors during most weeks of the summer. With its whimsical military theme and zany traditions, JBC has become *the* camp for a generation of campers that come to THE WILDS in North Carolina. Tim Meals (Major Meals) has directed the camp from its inaugural year.

Spiritual Emphasis Weeks

In the early days, these camps were called Outdoor Education or School Camps. Whatever the name by which it has been called, this program began with the rise of the Christian education movement in the early seventies and has run continually during the fall and spring months. THE WILDS has had the great joy of being a partner and enthusiastic cheerleader for Christian schools as they became numerous and prosperous. It is possible that the ministry of

THE WILDS sees as many Christian school student bodies as any nonschool organization in fundamental Christianity.

It is almost unimaginable to students that school can be held in such a healthy, wholesome environment where the students learn to love God and each other. Here they enjoy the preaching and teaching of God's Word as it relates to all the relationships of life. Here they enjoy the most fun a teen could conceive of and still call it school! What a way to go!

Senior Trips

Since the early seventies as an expansion of THE WILDS ministry with Christian schools, THE WILDS has hosted seniors for the trip that becomes the culmination of their high school career. This program was highjacked from public school settings in which students would go to a location and indulge the flesh, doing the opposite of what they were taught at home and at school.

At THE WILDS this is an all-star program where the seniors are honored with special meals and snacks, huge amounts of free time to enjoy the activities of the camp, a rafting trip, relevant messages, unique activities for making memories with the class, and most importantly, a Christ-honoring atmosphere where the great time is guilt free.

Historically, seven late spring weeks and one fall week are set aside for the mighty seniors who find a warm, fun-filled atmosphere. This atmosphere does not contradict the lessons of their education which has been carefully patterned around knowing, loving, and serving God. Senior trips are among the highlights of graduation from a Christian high school and one of the last and lasting memories of school and classmates—fun with no strings attached.

Camper-in-Training (CIT)

Since 1970 this program has progressed from one two-week session to three two-week sessions during the summer months. In the early days the program was under the direction of Major Ron Brooks. Soon Dr. Les Ollila and Dr. Marty Von forged an outstanding team to teach servant leadership to between fifty to seventy-five rising juniors and seniors in high school.

In more recent years Dr. Jim Berg, Dr. Sam Horn, and THE WILDS Director, Ken Collier, as well as staff members Scott Ashmore, Steve Stodola, and Matt Collier were added to the list of instructors. Dr. Matt Williams also helps as an instructor in the program.

It is very significant that well over fifty percent of THE WILDS staff members in any given summer have graduated from the CIT program. Campers who have attended THE WILDS from their very youngest years count their CIT session as the time when spiritual direction was set.

Music Conference

This program was begun in 1991 and has been a major source of encouragement to Christians servants involved in church and school music. The program is an oasis in the desert for people who wish to learn, share, and ask questions about how God is glorified in this critical aspect of life and ministry.

Is it controversial? Sometimes. It is an honest and biblical look at an area that can be emotionally charged, but an area that is so important to the life of Christ's church. The key sessions are handled by a senior pastor or an experienced evangelist.

Mac Lynch, Music Director at THE WILDS, and Tim Fisher, President of Sacred Music Services, had a great burden for this conference from the beginning of its existence. They do an excellent job of coordinating a program that brings eager people from across the country, and even the world, to sharpen their music skills for the glory of God.

Couples' Conferences

Since the early history of THE WILDS, Couples' Conferences have made a grand difference in several generations of married couples. From the early days when Dr. Walt Fremont's advice to ladies was to "feed the brute" to modern days of instruction with such teachers as Jim Berg and Greg Mazak, the Couples' Conferences are a place of serious learning and commitment for married couples young and old. The level of enjoyment at these retreats is sky-high. It is not unusual to see three generations of couples at a conference. What a wonderful tradition!

Pastors'/Youth Workers' Conferences

Since 1973, known earlier as the Youth Workers' FITness, these conferences have trained literally hundreds of full-time and lay youth workers in the philosophy and basics of the youth ministry. The program is always relevant and up-to-date because the speakers are men who have spent their lives working with young people and training others to do the same.

Since its inception, Ken Hay, Les Ollila, and Frank Hamrick have guided the program to meet the needs of today's and tomorrow's young people. There are separate tracks for pastors and for the wives of the youth workers. This conference is the longest-running program in fundamental circles specializing in the training of youth workers. A listing of God's servants in active ministry who have benefited from this program would be substantial and heartening.

These are only a few of the programs that the Lord has allowed THE WILDS to pioneer. Each program, no matter its size, is greatly loved. With the Lord's help the staff will continue to develop more All-Star programs to help God's children to be prepared and ready for the Master's use.

In Their Own WORDS

I was at the Leadership Conference last fall. God has really placed a burden on my heart for the mission field. I wish there were words to express the fullness that He has put in my heart. I so want God to be able to use me. My greatest fear is my flesh getting in the way of His holiness. "A Passion for Thee" has been my song for the past year. The first verse says, "Purge me from earth; turn my heart after Thine."

—*Camper*

My kids were at THE WILDS for a senior week of camp. I am a lay youth pastor, and I have never had the opportunity to set foot on your campsite, but I have seen the results in the hearts of young people these past fifteen years. This year the teens returned with a renewed spirit and mind. When young people bring back recorded messages and say, "Pastor, you gotta listen to this one," you know that they had a good week where decisions were made and God was honored. Thank you!

—*Youth pastor*

Chapter Nine

Buildings and Improvements That Made a Difference

ALL THY WORKS SHALL PRAISE THEE, O LORD; AND THY SAINTS SHALL BLESS THEE.

PSALM 145:10

Buildings do not build people. They shelter people who then have the privilege of hearing and doing God's Word from the heart, thereby growing. THE WILDS has been blessed with a functional and beautiful campsite with buildings that are a testimony to God and a credit to the sacrificial friends God has given the ministry. Through the years, God's people have rallied to the need for buildings and improvements that have made a great difference taking the ministry to the next level in both quality of experience and number of campers. Each one of the buildings on the campsite and in Taylors, South Carolina, has met important needs, starting with the original buildings, those "old-timers" at the campsite. The following buildings and surprising improvements have combined to make THE WILDS a place of impact for campers.

The Lowly Birdhouse

"Humble beginnings" would be an understatement when the original cabins at THE WILDS are discussed. Many parents, campers, and even staff members have been pointed the direction to the original cabins at THE WILDS, and then standing in front of them murmured, "You have got to be kidding me!"

Made from four-by-eight foot sheets of plywood, the eight-by-sixteen foot little cottages boasted a whopping one hundred twenty-eight square feet of "luxurious" living space with two closets boasting six feet of suitcase storage and clothes-hanging space for the seven campers and one counselor who occupied them. Each camper had a smidgen over sixteen square feet of living and breathing space, giving rise to the comment, "Those things were so small, you had to go outside to change your mind!"

The technologically advanced air-conditioning system (screened door in front, screened window in back) was only highlighted by the fashionably bare one hundred fifty watt bulb in the ceiling. Yet for all of their perceived weaknesses, they were much beloved by campers and staff members through several generations. Highly flexible, they even served as housing for couples during the Couples' Conferences in the early days. All one had to do was pile all eight mattresses in the back half of the birdhouse and you had a wall-to-wall bed that approximated queen size. The charm was there if the privacy was a little questionable.

The birdhouses were all retired with little fanfare, but great honor, in 1997, after twenty-eight years of continual service. They were replaced by comfortable and roomy duplex cabins consisting of three hundred ninety-six square feet for the boys and three hundred twenty-four square feet for the girls. What a radical change! For those who have to endure the luxury of the new cabins, try not to be envious of all those who had the opportunity to live in that icon of privilege—the birdhouse.

THE DORMITORY

"The Dorm," as it is lovingly referred to, is the plainest of buildings that has made one of the greatest impacts on the ministries of THE WILDS. The project of Bob Wilcoxen, the former Director of Development, and Walt Rumminger, a faithful board member of THE WILDS, the Dormitory was built in 1975. Before the Dorm was built, the camping season from September to May was severely short of rooms for guests. The summer cabins, which were unheated and open to the cold, could be inhabited only in early fall and late spring. This meant that only the twenty-one rooms in the Lodge could be counted on for guest lodging. Before the Dorm, a Ladies' or Men's Retreat could accommodate only about one hundred people. A Couples' Conference could accommodate only thirty-six people. A Teen Camp could pack in more, but not until the motel furniture was removed and bunk beds put in its place.

Enter the workhorse, the plain vanilla building known simply as *the Dorm*. For years the Dorm was used on weekends for couples and families. Although far from ideal for adults, its thirty-six rooms with an adequate male and a female bathroom on each hall more than doubled the weekend capacity. It made it possible to have Teen Camps throughout the year. As Spiritual Emphasis Weeks and Senior Trips gathered momentum, the Dorm gave convenient housing for teens.

In the first year the Dorm came into service, camp attendance went from five thousand to eight thousand for the year. Even today the husky and sturdy Dorm serves as the Barracks for the Junior Boot Camp campers. Be it ever so humble, the Dorm made a huge difference to the ministry of THE WILDS.

The Activity Center

Built in 1975 and dedicated to the memory of Coach H. Lee "Rock" Royer, the H. Lee "Rock" Royer Memorial Activity Center made an immediate impact on the camp program. The summer camps had outgrown the Fireplace Room of the Lodge, so the Activity Center became the auditorium for all services. During those frequent western North Carolina rainy weeks, the chairs were put away; and, for the first time in the seven-year the history of THE WILDS, there was an indoor place for campers to play group games. This was revolutionary for the program staff!

During the nonsummer months when cold and wet weather set in, the Activity Center saved the day as a hub of volleyball and basketball activity. In the summer it continues to be the preaching center, seating fourteen hundred campers, sponsors, staff, and visitors each evening. The Activity Center is one of the camp's best friends.

The Activity Center is one of the camp's best friends.

The Paving of Old Toxaway and Frozen Creek Roads

Although this paving does not fit the criteria for a *building* that made a difference in the ministry of THE WILDS, it is a magnificent feat of construction which every staff member and adult camper appreciates.

Did you ever have the privilege of driving the unpaved five-plus mile roads into the camp? The washboard effect would shake every bolt and clamp in any vehicle . . . in addition to any fillings in the passengers' teeth. On dry days dust was often several inches deep and powdery enough to find its way into any car's ventilation system. If one happened to be following a car into camp, the dust caused a total "brown-out" on the road, making visibility nearly impossible. One man said, "I wasn't *driving* my car down the road. I was aiming it!"

The unpaved roads were the scene of a number of fender benders. On rainy days the road seemed bottomless with thick, gooey mud which made the final five miles an extreme adventure. Camps that took place near the winter season were especially vulnerable to the fickle mud levels on the roads. On several occasions the old three-quarter-ton retired Army M-37 cargo carrier was used to pull church buses through the muck to the paved roads. Caretaker Marvin Lindgren and his young assistant Dave Cleary became extremely proficient as a wrecker crew.

After many pleas, petitions, and prayers, the North Carolina Department of Transportation announced that the roads would be paved at last. After the paving of both roads—Old Toxaway in 1986 and Frozen Creek in 1995—the final piece of this increasingly smooth puzzle was added when God's people graciously gave money to pave the interior roads and the parking lot in the main camp area.

Maybe somebody somewhere connected with the ministry of THE WILDS misses the graveled roads and parking lot . . . maybe. But most people are thrilled!

BLACK FLY TREATMENT

In what way can a little insect bring improvement to THE WILDS? Actually the camp was improved by the *absence* of these determined insects.

Doug Gorsline, the Landscape Supervisor at camp, took a pesticides-training class at Clemson University, where he had received his undergraduate degree. He brought a sample of the flies to the experts at the Entomology Department at Clemson who determined that the little culprits were black flies. He was told at the time there was nothing that could be done to interrupt the life cycle of black flies.

At that time the air at camp was thick with them at certain times of the year. They came in droves several times during the year and almost literally painted the area black. It was common during activity times to see staff members and campers with one hand held in the air, adopting the strategy that the diminutive pests would hover at the highest point. Everyone knew in their minds, however, that these little guys were partial to dive-bombing eyes, ears, mouths, and noses! Almost everyone referred to these tiny creatures as "those gnats." These aggressive flying specks were so bothersome that songs about them were written for Funtime.

Two years later Doug took an entomology class and went to the professor to discuss again the black flies at THE WILDS. That professor put him in touch with the right people who helped him devise a plan which did interrupt the life cycle of the black flies by treating the water in which they lay their eggs. It was decided that the Lake and the streams should be treated with an EPA-registered bacteria program. Since Clemson University was only fifty miles away, Doug was able to utilize the resources there, and for the past twenty-three years black flies have been controlled at THE WILDS.

The guy who discovered this bug-inhibiting bacteria should be in line for a Nobel Prize in the opinion of the loyal campers of THE WILDS who remember the plague of flies.

The Fremont Inn

On the site that once was a depository for broken cinder block and rusted metal a crown jewel was built for the ministry of THE WILDS. The Walter G. Fremont Inn was named to honor this original board member and the pioneer of Couples' Conferences at THE WILDS. The complex features a sixteen hundred square-foot Fremont Chapel (named after Dr. and Mrs. Walt Fremont) and a spacious, downstairs conference room called the Blue Ridge Room. The two separate wings of the Inn have fifty-two beautifully appointed rooms, a

Speaker's Suite, as well as laundry facilities for guests. The Fremont Inn is filled to capacity with the sponsors that come with the teen and junior campers during the summer. It is rare that there is a weekend when the Fremont Inn does not play a major part in the housing puzzle. In the nonsummer months the Inn allows for two separate programs to be run simultaneously. There can be a Couples' Retreat in the main camp area and a Deacons' Retreat in the Fremont Chapel at the same time.

The Inn was constructed through volunteer and full-time staff labor. Darrell Kidd of THE WILDS staff was the project manager and did an excellent organizing job. John Peery and Nelson Neal, board members of THE WILDS, organized a volunteer construction crew to frame the huge complex, including men from their own companies, Peery Construction Company and Advent Construction in Greenville, South Carolina. Destrie Shultz, a talented cabinetmaker, was responsible for the rich chair rail and crown molding in the corridors and conference areas.

The Fremont Inn has opened the door for greater numbers in our Couples', Family, and Senior Adult Camps. Camp life without this beautiful building is now unimaginable. The ministry was made stronger by the sacrificial gifts of time and money that made this lovely building possible.

The Dining Hall Porch

The porch was the brainchild of Rand Hummel. Three things must be available to be able to plan for expansion of camper numbers: there must be housing, there must be a place large enough to seat the crowd, and there must be room to feed campers. In the large expansion that came about in 2000, the logjam was in seating campers, sponsors, and staff at meals. Rand creatively rewrote schedules, and Rick Stoner configured new seating arrangements to allow junior high campers to eat during the early meal shift with sponsors and staff. A few years later Rand proposed the addition of a porch and deck onto the Dining Hall that would move the sponsors out of the noise and make room for the expanded numbers in the main dining room. In the nonsummer season the porch is a favorite place for rocking and talking for the many adults who come to the various conferences. It was an absolutely perfect plan at a perfect time.

THE LAKESIDE CENTER

A second full-scale camp and a dream from the very first master plan of THE WILDS was accomplished when the Junior Boot Camp (JBC) was opened in May of 2002. All of a sudden the ministry of the camp expanded by as many as two thousand campers through the junior program.

That would not have been possible without the addition of the Lakeside Center, which in the summer becomes the General Headquarters for the Junior Boot Camp. It was imperative that the JBC have a totally separate campsite, but remarkably it was planned to be near enough to the main camp to share eating facilities. Again Rand Hummel and Rick Stoner, Maintenance Director, were on the spot to determine how to house, schedule, and feed the new camp on the block. With amazing creativity and teamwork, the Junior Boot Camp occupies the Lakeside Center which serves the campers with an auditorium, PX (bookstore), snack shop, counseling room, infirmary, and game room. Steve Hill was the project manager for this versatile building. What a difference it has made in the ministry of THE WILDS.

LANDSCAPING AT THE WILDS

In the years prior to 1979, Herb Mueller, Diane Hay's father, managed the grounds. Even into his early eighties, he continued his amazing work in the camp landscaping. His specialty was roses, and at one time he maintained several rose beds with over four hundred rose bushes on the grounds of THE WILDS. The famous Perkin's Rose Company issued new varieties with which he could experiment. If he was unable to grow them, no one else could!

People always comment on the beautiful flower beds, the weed-free gardens, and the freshly-trimmed and cut grass.

Led by Doug Gorsline, our men keep the greenhouse producing and maintain the equipment. They trim back or take out unsightly trees, spray the campsite for unwanted insects, manage the flower beds, and blow and mow constantly. During the summer it takes eight strong men who are always toting, maintaining, pushing, riding, or fixing equipment to make THE WILDS one of the most manicured camps in the country.

People always comment on the beautiful flower beds, the weed-free gardens, and the freshly-trimmed and cut grass. One visitor said recently, "This place looks like a golf course!" Perhaps it's not that precise, but the intent is the same. The eleven-acre Ballfield is mowed every several days, giving it a fairway appearance—an amazing feat, keeping the grass growing with thousands of feet running, sliding, and stomping. The entire mile-long roadside from the front gate down to the Lodge is kept in beautiful condition. A couple of the staff men do little else than weed flower beds every day, and the steady drone of the Weed Eater is continual.

THE WILDS Office in Taylors, South Carolina

While nowhere near THE WILDS North Carolina campsite, this administrative office is located at 3209 Rutherford Road in Taylors, South Carolina. This location handles the corporate records, publications, information technology, product warehousing, shipping, camper registration, and other vital functions. Separated from the campsite by fifty miles, this attractive seventy-five hundred square-foot building was purchased and painstakingly redone by volunteer labor.

From its early beginnings in the basement of the Hay's home on Azalea Court in Greenville, the corporate office held up through two moves, one a rented facility, before it found the spacious building to purchase in this convenient location. This was a giant step in efficiency for the whole ministry of THE WILDS.

THE WILDS General Store

Beginning in 2010 a dream for many years will be realized when the new store and office complex will deliver the camp from several major inefficiencies. With summer numbers up to fourteen hundred a week, including staff, THE WILDS General Store with its twenty-five hundred square feet of space will relieve the stalwart Kountry Store with its four hundred five square feet of space. This is important, as one of the missions of THE WILDS is to bring families and individuals in contact with resources—books, recordings, and other remembrances—that will aid them in taking the next spiritual step in their growth towards Christlikeness.

In addition greatly needed office space will make the ministry much more efficient. More convenient public restroom facilities in this area of the main camp area will also greatly help. The expansion of the store will give more game room space in the Snack Shop area. This beautiful building will enhance the ministry is a variety of ways.

The Cool Beans Coffee Shoppe

Happy was the day when the idea of a small, full-service coffee shop at THE WILDS was considered and approved. Was a coffee shop frivolous, "nice but not necessary," a little over-the-top, not on the radar, or not even wanted by campers? As it turns out, the addition of the Cool Beans Coffee Shoppe in 2000 was an amazingly refreshing idea. This little spot away from the hustle and bustle of the activities is one of the more unique and spirited places on the campsite.

Undergoing an expansion in 2009 that nearly doubled the capacity, Cool Beans has won the hearts of many as the best place to relax and enjoy the company of friends. The creative Cool Bean's staff adds spirit to the camp by naming the ever-increasing varieties of drinks in recognition of the seasons, the speakers, and the activities. Cool Beans is "A Taste of THE WILDS."

In Their Own WORDS

My daughter went on her Senior Class Trip to THE WILDS and got saved. She came home a different person and is now headed to the medical mission field. Thank you!

—Mom, speaking with tears in her eyes

This past week was my Senior Class Trip. What an experience it was! To be honest, some of us were not looking forward to it. It turned out to be a great time of fun and fellowship. I know that many of my classmates, including myself, were really touched by the sermons and care the staff gave to us.

—Senior Trip camper

The humble Birdhouse—
the original cabins

The Birdhouse—cozy, but
comfortable living

Girls' Duplex Cabins

The Dormitory made a difference

The Dining Hall Porch—
a leap forward

The H. Lee "Rock" Royer
Memorial Activity Center

The Activity Center today

The old steps to the
Activity Center

The new, greatly improved steps
to the Activity Center

Groundbreaking for the Fremont Inn

The Walter G. Fremont Inn

THE WILDS General Store—the spiritual resource place

The Cool Beans Coffee Shoppe—the popular venue

Funtime with Tom Farrell, George Thornton, and Ken Collier

Willie Partin and Rand Hummel in Funtime

Funtime with "The King and I"—Jerry Dean and Ken Collier

Funtime—a tradition at THE WILDS

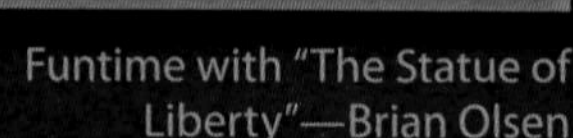

Funtime with "The Statue of Liberty"—Brian Olsen

Funtime with "The Kid"—Matt Herbster

Army-Navy Week festivities with Drum Major Ken Hay

Army-Navy Week with Coach Royer of the Navy team

Army-Navy Week with Major Ron Brooks of the Army team

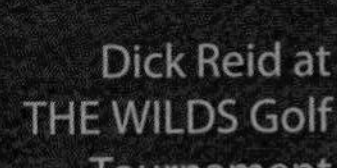

Dick Reid at THE WILDS Golf Tournament

Wilderness Camp at THE WILDS with Ray Shaffer, Dave Cleary, and Rick Stoner

Action at Junior Boot Camp Headquarters

Junior Boot Camp—a lasting impression

THE WILDS of New England with Director Rand Hummel

THE WILDS of New England in Deering, New Hampshire

THE WILDS of the Rockies—a spiritual landmark for many

THE WILDS of the Rockies on beautiful Lake Agnes in Kremmling, Colorado

CampsAbroad in Kenya, one of forty countries served

Excited campers in Papua, New Guinea

The Campfire Service in the 70s

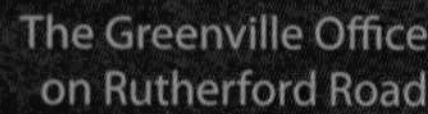

The Greenville Office
on Rutherford Road

THE WILDS Staff 1979

THE WILDS Staff 2009

Chapter Ten

"ABOVE ALL THAT WE ASK OR THINK"

> NOW UNTO HIM THAT IS ABLE TO DO EXCEEDING
> ABUNDANTLY ABOVE ALL THAT WE ASK OR THINK,
> ACCORDING TO THE POWER THAT WORKETH IN US,
> UNTO HIM BE GLORY IN THE CHURCH BY CHRIST JESUS
> THROUGHOUT ALL AGES, WORLD WITHOUT END. AMEN.
>
> EPHESIANS 3:20–21

One would think that a look at the history of THE WILDS would allow you to see what you expect to see, a camp in North Carolina that does . . . camp! By God's grace and through His direction, God has called upon THE WILDS ministry to give more to the cause of Christ than was imagined in those beginning years. The "higher ways" of God have presented multiple opportunities that flowed out of the simple desire to be useful to God in whatever ways He chooses, and what He has chosen has surprised and blessed the hearts of many. He has done "exceeding abundantly above all we that we ask or think." The following describe some of the programs that have naturally spun off from the wonderful ministry of camping at THE WILDS.

THE WILDS Evangelistic Team

For eleven years from 1979 until 1990 THE WILDS Evangelistic Team crisscrossed the country providing strong, fervent preaching and bright, conservative music. It was obvious early on that Tom Farrell was an evangelist whose gift from God should be exercised. The preaching at THE WILDS brought forth scores of invitations to come and partner with local church pastors to encourage Christians and minister to unbelievers. Tom and Regina, though carrying a heavy load at camp, were excited at the prospect of traveling and preaching with the ministry's blessings.

Seizing another opportunity to be a blessing to churches, it was decided to pursue a team concept, adding music to the makeup of the team. Mac Lynch was there from the beginning, first as a single man, and then in 1982 with his bride, Beth. Steve and Faye López traveled with the team for four years along with the single men who made up THE WILDS Quartet.

Several recordings from the team became all-time favorites of many. God greatly used this ministry for His glory. The team was dissolved in 1990 when Tom began the Tom Farrell Evangelistic Ministries.

Music Recording and Publications

From the earliest days of THE WILDS, good music was almost a byword. Beginning with Frank Garlock, the first Summer Music Director of THE WILDS, the succession line went to Ron "Patch" Hamilton, then to Steve López, and, after the ending of THE WILDS Evangelistic Team, to Mac Lynch. Mac's burden to help musicians and music programs in local churches was magnified by his own problems with the music of the world in his teen years.

Through Mac's leadership and with the help of Beth, Faye López, and many other godly musicians, THE WILDS became a leader in the emergence of refreshing, bright, conservative Christian music which gave Christians bona fide choices. The songbooks from THE WILDS (now in its seventh edition) have been used in churches, youth groups, and camps all over the country and even in foreign lands.

In 1986 Mac and Beth realized that there was a lack of choral sheet music, and they started a publishing arm of the music ministry which has encouraged a whole generation of musicians to begin to write Christ-honoring, conservative music.

While music was not in the original plans for THE WILDS, it was God's plan to encourage and challenge thousands of people and families in the critical area of Christian music.

THE WILDS OF THE ROCKIES

For seventeen years THE WILDS Christian Association had the incredible opportunity to minister to the local churches west of the Mississippi through THE WILDS of the Rockies, located in proximity to Rabbit Ears Pass and Muddy Pass near Kremmling, Colorado. The influence of that ministry has burned brightly in the lives of the many who trusted Christ and surrendered to His will at one of the most beautiful campsites ever developed in our country.

It is estimated that over thirty-six thousand campers attended THE WILDS of the Rockies. Operating from the same philosophy as that of THE WILDS in North Carolina, the camp with its dedicated staff added the scores of unique western touches that made it a most special place for hundreds of teens, many of whom are in the ministry today.

The camp ministered to lives "for such a time as this" until its closing in 2004. Those who loved this camp will never forget the trail rides, the flour fights, the hike to Baker Mountain, the picnics at the Meadow, the redoubtable wildlife, and the view from Rocky Point. For so many young people and adults, that view and the influence was, indeed, eternal. It does not take a long conversation to find out who the privileged ones were who attended this magnificent place. No need to ask. They will tell you. The experiences and the spiritual benefit will stay with them forever.

CampsAbroad

Who would have imagined that THE WILDS would be exporting its biblical philosophy of ministry, staff-training materials, activities, and Bible Study materials all over the world? Ken Hay had been doing this informally for many years through his ministry of consulting with national and international camps. But the burden came freshly to a young man, Matt Collier, who spent an undergraduate summer ministering at a camp in Australia. Matt, who had been reared at THE WILDS, recognized that groups of churches and mission groups overseas did not need men to come to the field to engage in full-time camp work. They needed a trained national who would take camping as an important part of his burden to reach nationals through the amazing tool of camping.

In 2001 CampsAbroad became an official arm of THE WILDS ministry, supported by an enthusiastic group of local churches and individuals. CampsAbroad has been to over forty countries encouraging "more camps . . . better camps . . . stronger camps abroad." All of the training and materials are provided to the foreign ministries abroad at no charge, and THE WILDS name is not placed on any camp ministry.

From a very humble beginning when Matt and Kelly Collier took trips alone, the ministry has developed to the point that numbers of

THE WILDS staff and leaders from sister camps have for the last several years averaged ten international trips each year. Camps are now strong in countries where there had been no camp ministries. In places where camp ministries already existed, they have been strengthened and energized with ideas, training, and biblical philosophy.

The influence of CampsAbroad is truly worldwide. To God be the glory!

The influence of CampsAbroad is truly worldwide. To God be the glory!

THE WILDS OF NEW ENGLAND

From what used to be a spiritual desert, new life springs in the form of exciting local church ministries in the area of our country's birth, New England. In 1999 a call came to THE WILDS from Leon Moody of Dublin, New Hampshire, representing a group of pastors in the New England area. Mountain View Bible Camp, which had served the Northeast with Christian camping, foresaw the closing of their camp in order to concentrate on the Christian boarding school, Dublin Christian Academy. The men asked if THE WILDS would consider a regional camp in New England. It was a captivating thought, but seemed a faraway possibility. Prayers were offered from that time on by staff and friends.

Then in 2002 a beautiful five hundred sixty-plus-acre tract of land was offered at a reasonable price by a Christian businessman. The property was near the historic town of Meredith, New Hampshire, on Lake Winnipesaukee. The Lord brought in the purchase price through the sacrificial giving of God's people, many from the New England area. The property was purchased, and it was determined that the development would begin after funds were provided, and not before. Securing permits to build a camp was a great challenge, and it was discovered that the property, though beautiful, was near enough to the town to bring a number of disadvantages for an active camp program such as is run by THE WILDS. And so in April of 2005 it was determined that the property would be sold. THE WILDS of New England needed to find a more remote home.

In 2007 the first week of camp for THE WILDS of New England was held for juniors at a rented facility, Singing Hills, near Lebanon, New Hampshire. One hundred forty-four campers gathered for a Junior Camp August 13–17. The camp was lead by the Director of THE WILDS of New England, Rand Hummel. The same arrangement was made in 2008, and the blessings of what God did in these short weeks began to mount.

In 2009 a great step of faith was taken. It was decided that THE WILDS of New England would run three weeks of Teen Camp and two weeks of Junior Camp at the Deering Center in Deering, New Hampshire. The opportunity to rent a good camp for five weeks of camp during prime summer-camping weeks was a wondrous thing. However, the wonder turned to puzzlement as the leaders of the Deering Center called to inform Rand Hummel and Dick Reid that the camp was not going to survive a financial crisis, putting the rental agreement into dire jeopardy. The leadership of the Deering Center asked if THE WILDS would consider assuming the mortgage.

Unfolding in rapid succession in the early months of 2009 was the sale of the property at Meredith and the purchase of the Deering Center. Rand Hummel, one of the most thoroughly knowledgeable, creative, and experienced staff members at THE WILDS, excitedly began to move forward in planning for five weeks of camp plus a Staff Training Week. The purchase of the Deering Center, which was to become the long-awaited THE WILDS of New England, was accomplished officially on March 19, 2009, almost ten years from the first inquiry. A WILDS camp was finally born to glorify God in the Northeast.

In Their Own WORDS

I want to thank you and your staff for the tremendous blessing that the Music Conference was to me and the other attendees from our church this past January. Words cannot express the treasures and benefits we received from attending the conference. Not only are we better equipped to serve in the area of music, but our hearts are better prepared to serve the Lord in whatever kind of ministry He requires of us. Please keep producing God-honoring music.

—Music Conference camper

I want to thank you and CampsAbroad for coming to my country. It was my first time to be a camper, and it was a great joy for me because I got saved. Here at camp I was around many who trusted and believed in Jesus. I'm almost afraid to go home because there are so many temptations to pull me down. I know that I will make it by God's grace and be the person God desires for me to be in this life.

—Camper from Zambia

Chapter Eleven

THE FAITHFUL FRIENDS

WE GIVE THANKS TO GOD AND THE FATHER OF OUR LORD JESUS CHRIST, PRAYING ALWAYS FOR YOU, SINCE WE HEARD OF YOUR FAITH IN CHRIST JESUS, AND OF THE LOVE WHICH YE HAVE TO ALL THE SAINTS,

COLOSSIANS 1:3–4

Imagine it being the first summer of camp for THE WILDS. A word-of-mouth campaign had gathered a number of registrations for the summer of 1969. Several churches were willing to make an announcement and give the new camp a try. However, the camp had no reputation; it was an unknown entity. The total charge for the week was twenty-five dollars. At that price perhaps people decided they could afford to take a chance! The purpose of the low price, of course, was to introduce the program to people who would enjoy the experience and, hopefully, tell others. It worked! Most parents realized they could not feed their teenage boy on twenty-five dollars a week. It was a bargain!

Volunteer finance man Bob Stoner was excited about the new ministry, but he was nonetheless concerned about the low, low price. His sound advice was much the same from the first day he volunteered to the day of his retirement from the staff. He said, "Gentlemen, we must charge enough to pay the bills. No one is going to be advantaged if we cannot pay the bills." Of course he was right.

There has always been a fine line between keeping the lowest price and still being able to pay the bills. God has always provided. However, since all fees and registration money go into the daily upkeep of the people and properties of THE WILDS, how was it possible to find extra finances to grow, build, and improve? The answer lies in the greatest gift possessed by THE WILDS—the gift of friends. Improvements and creative new projects would not happen without the faithful friends God has given THE WILDS.

The friends of THE WILDS are not just mildly interested parties. They are actually co-laborers in the ministry. True, they do not work daily at the office or the campsite, but these loyal and loving friends understand that the improvement of the ministry is an investment in the cause of Christ and His work. They have willingly interjected themselves into the heart of the ministry and have become as much a part of THE WILDS as the staff. The growth of THE WILDS through the years has been through the blessing of God knitting the hearts of friends to the ministry. Many of the exciting programs which have aided the ministry of THE WILDS have come through the suggestion of these friends.

THE SUSTAINERS

THE WILDS was in its first year when churches inquired about supporting the camp on a monthly basis. Realizing the constant pressure of ongoing financial obligations, they decided as congregations to make THE WILDS their camp, and they gave monthly to sustain the ministry in the day-to-day expenses. Soon individuals did the same thing, providing stability against those everyday working expenses. This group became known as the ministry Sustainers and many of them have been "at it" for forty-plus years. Others have joined in the roll of faithful Sustainers as soon as they learned about the ministry and its needs. Their prayers and sacrifices are consistent. It is humbling to be associated with this group of faithful helpers, old and new.

The Board

The twenty to thirty men and women who serve on the board of THE WILDS Christian Association, Inc. are gifted and faithful friends to the ministry coming from all walks of life. Board members are eligible to serve for two three-year terms and then must rotate off for one full year. They must heartily accept and sign the doctrinal statement of THE WILDS each year.

On the board are pastors and assistant pastors, business professionals, elected community officials, teachers, physicians, farmers, and Christian college administrators, to name a few. Many of their lives and the lives of their children have been touched by the ministry of THE WILDS. They faithfully attend the semiannual board meetings, but their interest and counsel to THE WILDS continues year-round. They are responsible for ensuring that the ministry stays within the framework of the doctrine and purposes for which THE WILDS came into existence. The wisdom God has given them has been critical in the low valleys and high mountaintops of the organization's history.

These men and women love God and the ministry of THE WILDS, and they have never been afraid to ask the hard question that might make the difference in the spiritual success or failure of the ministry. They are the good friends who offer strong accountability to THE WILDS.

SUMMER PARTNERS

The greatest expense to THE WILDS during the summer is also the greatest treasure. The expense is the salaries of the summer staff; the great treasure is the summer staff. Almost every one of the staff members are in the time of life with the greatest financial pressure they have ever known—the pressure of college expenses. Yet they come every summer and take the burden of the ministry on themselves. Staff members have the greatest summer of their lives and grow spiritually by leaps and bounds. They pray for God's provision to help them through school.

The greatest expense to THE WILDS during the summer is also the greatest treasure.

Knowing the magnitude of their sacrifice, the ministry wants to provide as much as possible financially. The salaries are not high, as one would expect with a volunteer ministry, but the available finances are also limited. Into that conundrum came a suggestion from board member Bob Garrett, who offered a plan in which churches and individuals could enter into a summer partnership with summer staff members, aiding them with prayer and aiding the ministry financially at the same time. Each Summer Partner would commit to pray for his summer staff partner and give toward his or her summer salary; and in exchange for the help and prayer, the summer staff member would contact his Summer Partner each week with a report of the blessings of the week and prayer requests for the coming week. In this way the burden of the salary to the ministry is relieved by the "many," and the proceeds can be funneled back into the ministry to meet expenses and to endeavor to keep the camp fees as low as possible and the salaries as generous as possible.

If there is such a thing as a "perfect storm," then maybe the Summer Partner Program could be known as the "perfect ministry blessing." Long-lasting friendships have been formed among partners young and old. The answers to prayers and the challenges of the summer staff members become present and personal to the Summer Partners. A banquet is held on a Saturday evening shortly past the halfway week in the summer at which time both Summer Partners (either a representative of the church or an individual) and summer staff members have the opportunity to meet and to encourage one another.

THE WILDS BANQUETS

Nearly every year staff members led by our Director of Development Dick Reid, hit the road to deliver a report on the progress of the ministry and to present the newest project that will help make the camp more effective in the lives of the campers. A nice meal is provided, and a voluntary love offering is taken to help with the expenses of the ministry.

The staff brings a little bit of camp with them sharing several music specials and often a humorous skit or two. Then a presentation is made for a project that is beyond the ability of the camp to provide, but one that will greatly enhance the enjoyment of the campers or meet a pressing need in the organization. The benefits and costs of the project are presented simply, and pledges are taken to complete the projects.

What has been accomplished through these informal times of giving and sharing? These banquets have been the means whereby almost all of the major buildings and improvements at THE WILDS have been made. The co-laborers and friends have been enabled by God to meet the needs time and time again in the history of THE WILDS.

THE WILDS GOLF TOURNAMENTS

Can anything good come out of the game of golf? Yes, many good things can and do come out of THE WILDS Golf Tournament, which is played in the fall of each year in the Greenville, South Carolina area. The captain's choice format and handicapping of individual's scores makes it possible for everyone to contribute to the team. Light-hearted banter at the auctions and silent auctions add to the good spirit of the occasion. Tournament sponsors, major sponsors, hole sponsors, and special event sponsors go out of their way to make the event a success.

Participants come from many different states to participate in a goodwill event that, among other good things, provides finances for the ministry to be able to offer scholarships to churches to bring at-risk young people to THE WILDS free of charge to the campers' families, who are seldom in the position to spend the money. These scholarships, coupled with the money which many churches give to help their own young people, give the assurance that unsaved young people have the chance to hear the gospel at THE WILDS. Through the generosity of many, chasing and hitting a little white ball has become an activity that strengthens the entire ministry of THE WILDS.

THE VOLUNTEER PROGRAMS

Helpers have come from many states, representing a burgeoning number of local churches and even businesses who volunteer to come to THE WILDS. These heroes to the ministry keep the maintenance, landscape, and building departments moving along productively. Everything from cleanup to stuffing envelopes to major building projects to car repairs have been conducted by the faithful volunteers who add energy and talent to the ministry.

Through the years, friends have found these ways and many others in which to express their support to the ministry of THE WILDS, which in turn keeps the ministry growing and strong. God has given THE WILDS many friends who co-labor with the staff to do the will of God. That is the greatest resource, humanly speaking, that THE WILDS has—our true-hearted friends. Sacrifice has been required; sacrifice has been cheerfully given.

In Their Own WORDS

The friendship and fellowship we experience at THE WILDS of the Rockies have always been a blessing and encouragement to us in strengthening our faith. After an excellent meal and entertainment performed by the staff on Saturday night, my heart was saddened as I realized this may be the last summer this incredible God-honoring ministry would be available to us in the West. The Holy Spirit of God shows His presence in an evening at THE WILDS stronger than any function I've ever attended. The staff performed their tasks professionally, and the whole program was like a well-oiled machine. No individual takes the credit; it is all to the glory of God.

—Friend of the ministry

It was at THE WILDS that God brought me to the place of complete surrender to Him. When I was the summer music director, Dr. Hay constantly encouraged me to compose music and to use my gifts for God's glory. As a result, many of my first songs were written at the camp. Over the years, I have made many trips to THE WILDS to get help developing the *Patch the Pirate Adventures* with my dear friend, Ken Collier. I could go on and on about attending various camps, making life-changing decisions, and seeking godly counsel and wisdom. How I thank God for THE WILDS!

—Ron "Patch" Hamilton

Chapter Twelve

FORTY-PLUS YEARS OF "FUNNY"

A MERRY HEART DOETH GOOD LIKE A MEDICINE:
BUT A BROKEN SPIRIT DRIETH THE BONES.

PROVERBS 17:22

Funtime at THE WILDS is somewhat of an institution in itself. Since the beginning of the history of the camp, there has always been at least a brief interlude of skits, scripts, and songs that bring laughter and "good, clean fun" to campers. In the first few years of camp, Funtime was held in the old Meeting Hall, the basement of the Dining Hall. It was small, cozy, stuffy, and incredibly hot, but the good spirit of the group always made it one of the most memorable times in any camping week.

In the course of time, the Fireplace Room became the Funtime venue. There was never a thought that holding Funtime in the same place where the services were held would be a problem. After all, *"Whether therefore ye eat, or drink, or whatsoever ye do, do* all *to the glory of God"* (1 Corinthians 10:31). Funtime is a time of serving campers and allowing them to see the staff in a different light—a very different light. As the summer crowds grew, the scope and sophistication of Funtime grew (if *sophistication* could be used in the same sentence with *Funtime*). With elaborate staging and lighting, teen Funtime has become quite a production. A Junior Boot Camp Funtime is also presented in the Lakeside Center each week.

Being funny is actually serious business, as anyone who has been a part of it would concur. Hours of work goes into each effort to appear spontaneous—and very dumb. Some do it better than others, but everyone taking part in the program has the opportunity to try. While everyone who appears in Funtime will be funny in their special role, there is usually one person who wins the heart of everyone.

Some people are more naturally funny than others. It may be an uninhibited personality. It may be natural timing. It may be a "rubber" face. It may be an interest in humor or a natural love of life. That is where the mystery and excitement lies. Who will become the Funny Man—the one that cracks everybody up? It is hard, if not impossible, to predict. But one thing is for sure; the campers will end up making that decision clear.

Along with the main Funny Man, there has to be one or more men who are his foil—his "Straight Man." The Straight Man feeds lines to his partner who replies with humorous quips. The Straight Man is sometimes the antagonist and appears humorless and insensitive so the Funny Man can shine. At THE WILDS there have been over forty years of funny men and straight men. How many do you old-timers and "new-timers" remember?

1969–1973: Jerry Dean and Ken Collier

Jerry Dean was at times shy in his personality, but he had a natural knack for making people laugh. His pantomime of "The Baseball

Pitcher" and "The Horse" are legendary at THE WILDS. He was a hit with "The Littlest Texan," featuring the expressive hands of Jerry Sprout, the first Program Director. Jerry Dean and Ken introduced the long-running three-act play, "The King and I." With Ken as the Straight Man, Jerry was an expert at Abbott and Costello routines such as "Who's on First" and "Fodder." His double takes and clueless looks took no prisoners. Everyone had to laugh.

Funtime is a time of serving campers and allowing them to see the staff in a different light—a very different light.

1974–1978: GEORGE THORNTON AND KEN COLLIER

George Thornton is 6'4" and has a wonderful sense of humor. He was so well-read that he had amazingly funny lines remembered from other ages of comedy. His specialty was monologues. His rendition of country comedian Jerry Clower was legendary, especially the story of the "Coon Hunt" ("Knock him out, John") that sent even teen audiences into spasms. His original monologue of his girlfriend Zelda was ridiculously funny at all times. George and Ken did a number of Abbott and Costello routines featuring George as the wide-eyed and often frustrated Funny Man.

1978–1985: KEN COLLIER AND RAND HUMMEL

Ken enjoyed doing word mix-ups like "Beeping Slooty," "We've Been Everywhere," "Bacon and Eggs," "What Have You Done for Me Lately?," "Bill McCluskey," "Fifty Favorite Parent Sayings," "I'm My Own Grandpa," and others. Ken and Rand formed a tight team together with Abbott and Costello routines and a new spoof called "Knotholes." Ken and Rand introduced a new skit that would become a signature for funny men of the future entitled "The Statue of Liberty." The "Banana Bandana" slapstick routine was among the ultimate funny gross-outs.

1985–1990: John Sheffield and Rand Hummel

John Sheffield raised the habit of laughing at his own jokes to an art form. He was able to get everyone laughing by laughing at himself, and he did so on almost every occasion. His dialogues with Rand were legendary, including "The Statue of Liberty," "Zelda," "John Henry," and others. His renditions of the old Smothers Brothers routines made him a sure thing in any Funtime. His collection of "Inventions" became classic. Rand, more often than not, accompanied him on guitar and was the exasperated brother.

1990–1998: Brian Olson and Rand Hummel

Brian Olson had a "rubber face" by any definition. His wide-eyed, blank look before a skit even started would send most audiences into gales of laughter. Skits got longer and longer because no character was able to continue while the audience refused to stop laughing. Brian brought the old Smothers Brothers routines to another level. He sold his character so well that people would believe it was his personality. His character in the musical "Jingle Cats" showcased his classic looks and could almost send an audience into convulsions. Rand's teamwork with Brian was the best mix of humor imaginable. They would never have taken a demotion from ministry in order to entertain, but they could have made any audience anywhere breakup with laughter.

> Being funny is serious business to the servants at THE WILDS

1998–2008: Willie Partin and Rand Hummel

Willie Partin was a likeable guy, so everyone liked him. He had a natural openness that brought an audience in with him immediately. They were ready to identify with him and liked anything he did within a very few minutes. Willie took up the mantle and did the variety of skits done by his predecessors, including "Inventions," Smothers Brothers routines, "The Fly," "The Cooking Show," and many others. He and Rand formed a solid team that won the hearts of the audience.

2008–PRESENT: WILLIE PARTIN WITH MATT HERBSTER AND SCOTT ASHMORE

This is not to say that the men who provide the background to the Funny Man are not funny themselves. Matt is a big man, so his size adds so much contrast to skits when he acts smaller than he is. Scott is the cerebral comic, using subtlety and timing to bring about big laughs. But there is still Willie who became the "everyman" hero. People put themselves in his place and enjoy looking at themselves in their most embarrassing moments.

The purpose of Funtime is to build bridges to the lives of campers and to break down barriers that would hinder the communication of God's Truth. Funtime is one of the sharpest tools in the bag of the servants who love campers and want to see them take the next step spiritually.

Being funny is serious business to the servants at THE WILDS.

In Their Own WORDS

When we announced to the parents and teens where we were planning to go for camp, the staff met with considerable static and skepticism. The teens all had their excuses. They arrived at camp ready to have a mediocre time, but when Friday rolled around, a one hundred eighty-degree change had taken place in each of their hearts. Now the campers from our church were begging to stay another week. Thank you for your faithfulness, and you can count on seeing us again next summer.

—Assistant pastor

I dedicated my life to the Lord as a senior at THE WILDS and thought that I would share with you what God has been doing since that time. I have been in full-time ministry as a youth pastor since graduating in 1995 from a Christian college. I am currently being sent out by my home church to plant churches to the unreached in Peru as soon as I have our support raised. Thank you for your time and part in helping to prepare me to give the gospel to the unreached.

—Missionary in South America

Chapter Thirteen

METEORS AND COMETS

TO EVERY THING THERE IS A SEASON, AND A TIME TO EVERY PURPOSE UNDER THE HEAVEN.

ECCLESIASTES 3:1

Almost everyone enjoys the light show of a meteor shower or the once-a-generation appearance of a comet when it pays its extremely rare visit to our little corner of the solar system. THE WILDS ministry has had many programs and concepts which rose quickly and burned brightly and beautifully. Although for one reason or another they did not pass the test of time, some longtime friends loved them, and they hold a place of affection in the memory. Here are some of the meteors and comets in the history of THE WILDS.

CHRISTMAS RETREAT

After Christmas would seem to be a perfect time for camp, and for many years it was for THE WILDS. This camp had a tremendous following, always full to running over. The young people were bristling with energy and enthusiasm. Having spent enough downtime at Christmas break, they were looking for something to do. The weather was always precarious, and while snow was always the hope for the many young people of the Southeast, it was more likely that they received very cold rain and sleet.

What happened to the Christmas Retreat? Once THE WILDS became a year-round camp, the staff of THE WILDS relied on this time of year as a genuine, purposeful recovery time with their families after the rigors of the full schedule. The planning and running of the Christmas Retreat meant that Christmas Eve and Christmas Day was generally spent preparing for the camp to come. It was decided that this time would be best blocked out as an unrushed family time.

In its place is now the Music Conference which begins close to the first of each calendar year. This is the time when many people involved in music can attend, and it allows THE WILDS staff to spend Christmas with family.

The Christmas Retreat holds many wonderful memories for those who came and those who worked.

Games That Were Great . . . at the Time

The Tarp

Imagine a rubberized nylon tarp about sixteen feet in diameter. It resembled a big, hand-held trampoline. Rope configured to act as handholds circle the entire tarp. Holding onto the rope are about twenty senior high teens and college men. On the tarp is a junior high boy or girl chosen for the fact that he or she weighs less than one hundred pounds. Now listen as the tarp holders begin to get in sync, letting the tarp go loose and then carefully tightening it, making sure that the one in the middle does not lose contact with the tarp. When all of the tossers seem to be moving in unison, the leaders begins the count: *one . . . two . . .* On *three*, the tossers pull as hard as they can, snapping the trampoline-like tarp tight, putting all of their muscles into it. The one in the center is launched sometimes twenty-five or thirty feet in the air. The look on the face of the "tossee" is priceless. The boys standing around the tarp give a cheer as they brace their feet to catch the erstwhile astronaut as he free-falls. If everyone doing the tossing pulled evenly, the one tossed returns perfectly to the center of the tarp. However, on those occasions when one side of the tarp was not as strong or not as synchronized as the other, quick-thinking catchers would walk the tarp to a place where catching the high-flying camper was assured.

The tarp could even be used inside the Fireplace Room on rainy days. Several teens got close enough to the ceiling to examine the nail holes. This was bold fun, breathtaking fun—too much fun and not quite enough margin for error. Trained firemen can do the task better, so the art of tarp tossing was retired. As Diane Hay once commented, "All of the guardian angels in the world were watching over us in those early days."

THE GARBAGE-BAG RELAY

Just as the tarp was not for the faint of heart, this relay was not for the faint of stomach. There were two teams lined up equidistant from two chairs. Underneath each chair was an innocent-looking paper bag folded over nicely. The object of the game was simple. On the whistle, the first of four participants on each team would run to the chair, sit down, reach under the chair and grab the paper bag, open the bag, eat or drink the contents of the bag, and then run back to tag his next teammate who would repeat the same action. If the fourth teammate finished the contents of the bag and ran back across the finish line first, his team was declared the winner.

> Wait a minute! What could be the harm in a simple relay like this?

Wait a minute! What could be the harm in a simple relay like this? The surprise was not in the object of the game, but in the objects which were in the bag. There was a reason it was called the Garbage-Bag Relay. The first participant might reach under the chair, open the bag, and grab a not-so-beautiful but oh-so-ripe black banana. Of course, bananas are not intended to be eaten when they are black, unless you are in a Garbage-Bag Relay. The next contestant might have to "chug" a pint jar of dill pickles—juice and all. The next contestant might pull out an onion, which could taste like an apple if one's imagination is vivid enough or if his gag reflexes could be fooled. The last contestant having seen the fate of the first three contestants might wonder if the bagged treats could get worse as the game gets closer to the end, and he was right. Can you imagine his expression after pulling out a jar of infant baby food correctly labeled "Beets and Strained Squash?"

What killed the Garbage-Bag Relay? It was done in by threats from the camp nurses.

People-Powered Drag Races

What could be more exciting to some people than the roar of the engine as the high-powered dragster roars down the track? THE WILDS had its own drag races. The engines were quiet, almost like they were not running, because they were not. These dragsters were people-powered. On the whistle each team would get as many teammates on the old nonperforming cars as possible and push them sixty or seventy yards to the finish line. The cars would fairly jump off the line; but the long race and heavy cars took their toll as human engines tired, and human feet got tangled together, and bodies went down in heaps, much to the delight of the campers watching from the not-so-grand stands.

No one will admit who came up with the idea to race the cars around markers strategically located around the Ballfield. This would likely be one of the zaniest relay races of all times. Could there be a slight problem having cars with human engines racing to see which would be the first to get around a distant pole and then come back to a finish line? Perhaps. So the racing season was cancelled before most of the current NASCAR drivers were racing tricycles.

Inner Tube Races

Let's see. You have a truck-tire inner tube and a long and steep hill. You have just finished tubing in the creek for the third time and are looking for something enterprising to do. What could be more fun than straddling the inner tube on the inside with your head inside the tube? Your arms push hard against the top of the tube. Now all you have to do is go to the top of the hill, push off, lift up your feet, and you become a runaway one-wheeled truck flying down the hill. Watch out now; there are bumps in the road that sometimes cause you to lose balance inside the tire, along with the disorientation of spinning three hundred sixty degrees two or three times a second. This activity was loads of fun for spectators, especially watching the rollers attempting to walk after the roll. For the rollers, it was fun as long as it lasted or as long as their feet, arms, and head stayed in the tube. This activity was so much fun, it became the poster child for "Don't try this at home!" and was banned at THE WILDS.

These are not the only activities and games that did not make the cut at THE WILDS. There are dozens of activities that were tried and found wanting for some reason or another. They were the meteors and comets of our game and activity world, and may they rest in peace!

The Wilderness Program

From 1972 to 1992 THE WILDS ran summer Wilderness Camps with most sessions lasting two weeks. The first week would be training in outdoor skills at a base or static camp, and the second week would be a challenging wilderness hike putting those skills to good use. There was even a one-night "solo" in which each boy—who became known as "Joe Wilderness" no matter what his city name—had to survive totally on his own. It was a tough regimen headed by Life Scout Rick Stoner and military veteran, Dave Cleary. Fellow veteran and nurse, Ray Shaffer provided medical help to the boys (blisters in abundance). The program toughened up many young men who were fiercely loyal to the program, but it was phased out because it was extremely labor intensive for the whole staff. The expansion of the teen program called for the talents of all the leaders back at the main camp. There is always talk of resurrecting this unique program. It was greatly loved and possessed stories of which legends are made!

The Honda Odysseys

Long before Honda had a family vehicle by this name, there was a four-wheel-drive buggy by this name, complete with racing harnesses and roll cage. It was decided that it would be an exciting activity for high school seniors and adults who came to camp. True to its billing the Honda Odyssey ATV carts were exciting, but the immensity of the excitement for the supervising and maintenance staff could not have been reckoned. Each trip out to THE WILDS outback featured a trained staff member in the lead and tail vehicle. The group had to be kept reasonably close on the mountain trails for safety's sake. What was not apparent to most of the inexperienced drivers was the difference between the brake on the steering wheel, as well as the accelerator, which was also on the steering wheel. The vehicles, which were extremely safe, nonetheless tended to disappear over the sides of the roads into the valleys below when under the guidance of inexperienced and overly-enthusiastic drivers. They also tended to slam into one another when the "gas" was mistaken for the brake. Sometimes it was a question as to whether the accelerator and brake were actually mistaken or whether the intent was to enjoy a "bumper car" experience. Many trees on the back trails still carry the scars. Staff member Jim Oswald was a very patient man and became very experienced with body work for ATVs.

It was a great idea . . . at the time, but the campsite might not have survived extended years with the Odysseys.

It was a great idea . . . at the time, but the campsite might not have survived extended years with the Odysseys.

ARMY-NAVY WEEK

For one week during the summers from 1971 to 1974 there was a week of camp like no other. The regular team names were set aside, and everyone became either Army or Navy. Thus was kicked off a week of pageantry that culminated in an actual Army-Navy Flag Football Game, an Army and Navy Queen with her court, cheerleaders, team floats, and even a marching band lead by distinguished Drum Major Ken Hay, twirling a fiery baton (a twelve-foot cardboard carpet roll set on fire).

Coach H. Lee "Rock" Royer was the Defensive Coordinator for the U.S. Navy Football Team, and Army Major Ron Brooks was recently back from flying helicopter combat missions in the Vietnam War. These men led the Navy and Army teams respectively. After the death of Coach Royer in a plane crash in November of 1973, the tradition continued for a few more years with former all-American Navy quarterback, John Cartwright, and former Army Football Team captain, Bill Hawkins.

This unique summer week is chronicled in Ken Hay's words in appendix D. As the sizes and numbers of camping weeks expanded, Army-Navy Week was set aside to preserve the strength and health of the staff. Those weeks were fun and served a delightful purpose for those golden years.

IGMO Club

In the seventies, a camper club called the IGMO Club was brought into being by Ken Collier, who was the Program Director at that time. The club was composed of campers who wanted to give to a project that would make the campsite more enjoyable for others campers. The campers received a newsletter just for them that gave an inside look at the planning of the program. The IGMO members and staff members became pen pals. What about the name IGMO? It was an acrostic meaning I Give Monthly.

Although the club was always small, several cheery projects were partially paid for by the club. There was a quality concessions wagon called the IGMObile that allowed campers to purchase treats on the field level. There was a deck behind the Snack Shop on which campers could relax, paid for by the IGMO Club. Its name? Why the IGMOdeck, of course!

Jerry Dean, the next Program Director, was in charge of the club for a number of years, and it expanded under his leadership. It was replaced by a regular article in THE WILDS Newsletter entitled, "For Campers Only."

The Camp Director's Institute

For five years, from 1977 to 1982, there was a one year, nonacademic certificate program of instruction called the Camp Director's Institute. Students worked off their tuition by providing the staffing for the fall through spring season. Up to eight students were allowed.

In the event the man was married, his wife was also able to work on the campsite. There were classes on the beginning days of camp and everyday classes during the winter months. Each department head had a block class during the year to cover every area of camping. Ken Collier was the main instructor in the administrative area with strong input from Ken Hay. Each student had to turn in a final project in which he designed a camp from the ground up, including site selection and financing. The students also benefited from a number of field trips to both secular and Christian camps throughout the Southeast. The program was always filled with eager men, and it was of great benefit to them as it also sharpened the ministry of THE WILDS. The time constraints of year-round camping forced a difficult decision to lay aside the program. Graduates included Rand Hummel, Marty Herron (former director at Northland Camp), Dan Nelson, Bill Ertel, Steve López, and other good men who remain good friends of the ministry.

These along with other programs and ideas make up what could be considered as the meteors and comets of THE WILDS. They were bright and beautiful in their time and purposeful for the ministry. We learned much and enjoyed the relationships brought about by God who made us wiser and richer spiritually through them. But, as with many other things in life, they were beneficial "for such a time as this." They served the needs of the day effectively and were retired with gratefulness and honor.

In Their Own WORDS

As I look back, I can gauge my spiritual growth from year to year at THE WILDS. I made major decisions there that did stick with me. I learned to have meaningful quiet times with God at THE WILDS. Being from the big city (Detroit suburbs), I will always cherish discussions I had with God on the bridge over the creek or on the hill overlooking the camp. I remember spiritual discussions with my counselors outside the birdhouse cabins. I learned to love the Word of God, and now I am a pastor and teacher, sharing God's Word with others. I would not be where I am today without the influence of THE WILDS in my life.

—Former camper, now pastor and teacher

Each year our children come home, not only with memories of fun, but with a deeper knowledge of God's Word. Of course, our son loves the menus too. It is such a blessing to have a spirit-filled and God-honoring camp for our young people. Thank you for your ministry.

—Parent

This was my second visit to THE WILDS, and I found it more rewarding than any youth camp that I have ever attended. The organization of the daily services were expertly arranged to provide the highest quality of Bible teaching while rendering the campers a great amount of time for activities. The entertainment and games with competition were well-planned and supervised by your staff throughout the week. Our week at THE WILDS will be remembered for many years.

—Pastor

Chapter Fourteen

"KEEPER" TRADITIONS, MAXIMS, AND CONCEPTS

I WILL REMEMBER THE WORKS OF THE LORD: SURELY I WILL REMEMBER THY WONDERS OF OLD.
I WILL MEDITATE ALSO OF ALL THY WORK, AND TALK OF THY DOINGS.

PSALM 77:11–12

Every place has their traditions, favorite sayings, and most-loved concepts. THE WILDS is heavily laden with traditions that are greatly loved and ingrained in our thinking. Some traditions began at THE WILDS; but some, no doubt, were learned in another place and time and by virtue of constant use became associated with THE WILDS. Regardless of where they came from, these traditions are a valued and sometimes whimsical part of camp life. Here are a few of the keepers from the storehouse of the culture of THE WILDS.

Campfire Service

This is camp tradition for many camps, but hardly a week goes by in which someone fails to express appreciation for the emphasis of the Campfire Service, which is a visual testimony of what the Lord has done in his or her life at THE WILDS.

Cabin Cheers

Of course this is not a new concept to camp, but THE WILDS has raised the concept to new levels of spirit . . . and decibels. During at least two meals each day, campers can cheer for their cabin and team. Our campers are committed cheerers and the later in the week, the louder the cheers! Through the cheers at camp, THE WILDS seeks to inspire every individual to join in and applaud a common cause. Through the lessons learned from the campers attaching themselves to a team with participation and spirit, some campers can understand the importance of going home and attaching themselves in a more-committed way to the greatest cause, that of living for Christ. The standard applied by THE WILDS to cheering is that it should draw focus to the team, not to those doing the cheering. Accordingly the staff is trained to glorify God by making proper choices in the cheers and choosing cheers that give the right opinion of God. Psalm 19:14 is to be considered when cheering: "*Let the words of my mouth, and the meditation of my heart, be acceptable in Thy sight, O LORD, my strength, and my redeemer.*" Cheering is fun, and remembrances of cabin and team cheers trigger memories for a lifetime.

The Steps

No matter how you slice it, the steps at THE WILDS are one of the main features always talked about before the camp week, during the camp week, and after the camp week. The steps even make it into the sermon illustrations of many speakers at camp. Some campers admit to training at home in preparation for tackling the steps at THE WILDS.

Someone once suggested an escalator fund where interested people could give towards the purchase of those moving stairs to help campers in the exercise of climbing the steps numerous times a day. After forty-plus years, the fund still sits at approximately $.53. Everyone knows the steps are the landmark to talk about and murmur about. But they are, after all, part of THE WILDS. The steps will not be moving any time soon!

THE FUNTIME

Funtime, as it is affectionately called, is a compilation of skits, songs, slapstick, and silliness providing a full hour of hilarity for campers and sponsors. It is hard to find campers who do not love Funtime. The goal is to get the campers to laugh at the skits, which are not vulgar, blasphemous, or immoral, but rather fall into the category of "good, clean fun" that can be performed to the glory of God. Funtime is truly a barrier-breaking and bridge-building time, allowing the campers to see that the staff members are real and approachable people who can be silly with the best of them. Being front and center in this oftentimes exaggerated and ridiculous way allows the staff members to humble themselves and serve the campers uniquely. Campers see the effort and appreciate it. Funtime greatly adds to the spirit of camp. Later on, that same staff member may be the one who preaches, teaches, sings, or in some other way challenges campers to growth in Christlikeness. Funtime is an outpouring of a refreshing life in Christ. Where do those crazy skits and songs come from? They are begged, borrowed, stolen, created, revamped, and recycled, but they are always loved.

Funtime is an outpouring of a refreshing life in Christ.

A Two-Way Rescue

This phrase originated from an illustration given by Ken Hay telling the story of a counselor who, while endeavoring to reach a camper for Christ, was herself changed and helped in the end. This is true of almost every staff member's experience who has worked at THE WILDS. We are all part of a two-way rescue.

God & I Time

The concept of a "personal devotional time" or "quiet time" is often used in camps, schools, and homes. However, this has been a forty-plus year burden in the heart and life of the founder, Ken Hay. (Dr. Hay, we got your life message, and it was a life-changing one.)

If there is one habit to ingrain in the lives of each camper, the godly habit of God & I Time would be the most important one. (Former campers, how is your God & I Time?) This is one of the enduring legacies left by the ministry of THE WILDS among us.

Maxims

"Put it in writing." This maxim is mentioned first because it is embedded in the heart of the founder. Why we do what we do should be written for all to see, study, learn by, and keep.

"Make it hard to sin and easy to do right." Rand Hummel admonishes thousands of teens with this maxim. If we would do this faithfully, we would excel for the Lord.

"There are just two choices on the shelf, pleasing God or pleasing self." Ken Collier admonishes campers to make choices with love for God and others in mind.

"We cannot rest on past successes. We need a fresh enduement of God's power in our lives." This is one of the founder's maxims, admonishing the staff to depend on God and not on self.

"Make up your mind." Dr. Walt Fremont, an original supporter and prayer warrior of THE WILDS, would emphatically plead for this with couples whose marriages were in trouble or who were suffering from a lack of spiritual growth. Some things had to be decided in the heart once and for all. You need to "make up your mind" to obey the Bible.

"The man who dies with the dirtiest towel wins." Ken Collier encourages campers to become like Christ by becoming a servant—"laying down your crowns, picking up a towel, and washing dirty feet of those around you by humbly serving them."

"Remember, safety is no accident!" Although it is not original with him, Rick Stoner brings this message across better than the originators, and it is one good reason why THE WILDS is a careful and safe environment.

"And if you want to hold a hand (*clap*)—hold your own!" This is Rand Hummel's well-known phrase from hundreds of teen orientation times, emphasizing to campers there is to be "no physical contact." His whimsical look at serious rules is the spoonful of sugar that helps the medicine go down.

"Be FEPI." Ken Hay often used this admonition to all staff members, encouraging them to become a staff member who is "Flexible, Energetic, Persevering, and Ingenious." Come on now, be FEPI!

"If God calls you to stand on your head and stack greased BBs, you ought to believe that He will give you the ability to stand on your head and stack greased BBs." Founder Ken Hay gave thousands of teens pause for thinking with this startling statement. Although the word picture was almost comical, it got the point across that "God can give you the ability to do anything He calls you to do." One summer's staff presented Ken with a homemade trophy of a little character standing on his head with a string of standing BBs beside him.

"Clean as you go." This is one of the maxims of Cal Mair, the Food Service Manager, and another reason why the kitchen at THE WILDS is a place of order, cleanliness, and delicious food. Seeing this phrase on the Galley staff (caps or shirts) just serves to reinforce the importance of its sparkling clean meaning.

"Hit it and follow it!" These are the instructions for how to win a Bigball game, as given in so many words by lead counselors throughout the history of THE WILDS.

"And I have one question . . . who is going to win this week?" This is the stock phrase used by program directors to cause staff members and summer campers to break into hysterical cheering . . . on cue.

"Six of one, half dozen of the other." Although this is not an original phrase, when it is said by Dave Cleary, longtime staff member, first aid expert, goodwill ambassador to the locals, vehicle repairman, and friend of sponsors, it means, "We are going to be flexible here. God has got everything under control."

"We've got five thirties today!" Cabin inspection is a forty-year tradition at THE WILDS. It is impossible to remember why the scale for a perfectly clean cabin for the morning inspection is thirty, but it has been that way from the beginning! Campers literally get down on hands and knees to scour the floor and porch in an effort to bag a thirty in the inspection. It is a cabin's great achievement.

In Their Own WORDS

I attended camp many times as a teenager and every time I went to camp, the Lord spoke to me. I surrendered my life to the Lord at the fireplace in the Lodge, and I knew He had called me to serve in some church ministry. The lessons I learned at THE WILDS come back to me daily. I can hear the saying "Just two choices on the shelf, pleasing God or pleasing self" guiding some of my decisions. When I shop for clothes, I hear, "Let the arrows of your fashion point to your face." As I see the broken lives of those I counsel, I recall, "You can choose your sin, but you cannot choose the consequences of your sin." As you can see, I have never forgotten what God imprinted upon my heart up there on the mountaintop. I pray you will continue to touch and make a difference in lives of people.

—Former camper

I experienced THE WILDS as a thirteen-year-old camper in 1973 and returned in 1974. I remember well the Tuesday evening service that second year. We were in the Fireplace Room, and I was sitting with my cabin mates. Dr. Ken Hay preached that night on repentance. It was as if I was the only one in the room. God showed me plainly that I had never repented of my sin, and all my trying to do "good" was not keeping me from failing. I went forward and was saved on August 12th that year. The next day I found out that almost half of our youth group had been saved in that service. Thursday of that week we went soul winning in Asheville, North Carolina. God was truly changing us. Later God led me to a Christian college and into the youth ministry. I am forever indebted to Dr. Hay and THE WILDS staff for the input they have had in my life, my family, and our youth. To God be the glory, great things He hath done.

—Former camper, now youth pastor

Chapter Fifteen
OUR HISTORY AND OUR FUTURE

BUT CONTINUE THOU IN THE THINGS WHICH
THOU HAST LEARNED AND HAST BEEN ASSURED OF,
KNOWING OF WHOM THOU HAST LEARNED THEM.

2 TIMOTHY 3:14

In the year 2006, a group of staff members, representative of three distinct generations of servants who minister at THE WILDS, met together. Their task was not an easy one, but it was by no means an unpleasant one. They were challenged to think of their association with the ministry of THE WILDS from the earliest they could remember to that present day and find the essential and enduring values that seem to have been true of THE WILDS all the way through. They were to identify and record that small set of guiding principles which are authentically believed by staff members, campers, and friends who have come to the camp throughout the years.

These values, known as THE WILDS Core Values, should not change with the generations. They should be true of this ministry fifty years from now or a hundred years from now, if the Lord were to delay His coming. We hope that these core values resonate with you, because many of you helped in their development—knowingly or unknowingly. With hopefulness for the future, continual prayer in every heart, and by the grace of God alone, may THE WILDS always be known for these six core values that are at the core of the ministry.

1. Faithful to the Bible

THE WILDS, as an organization made up of growing Christians, will be searching through, submissive to, and obedient to God's Word, the Bible. Strong preaching and teaching of this Word will be a central focus at THE WILDS. God & I Time, even if the name were for some reason changed, will be the godly habit that will make the most difference in the lives of every staff member and camper. Faithfulness to the Bible means memorizing the Bible and using it exclusively for teaching the next step for salvation or spiritual growth. THE WILDS must be faithful to the Bible and look to it in order to explain the needs of all men. We believe that if the Bible were written today God would need to say nothing new, nothing more, nothing less, and nothing different than what He already said in His true Revelation. It tells us what is most important for life and godliness. It tells us what is right. THE WILDS will always be ruled by an ancient Book which is alive and relevant to every person who has ever come, or who will ever come, to THE WILDS beautiful campsite.

Scores of men and women who have handled the Word of God carefully and faithfully have been used to make an unforgettable impact on lives of campers in the ministry of THE WILDS. Although the list is extensive and not all of the excellent speakers are listed, here are some of the more familiar ones who have preached and taught repeatedly at THE WILDS: Ken and Diane Hay, George Jensen, Walt and Trudy Fremont, Les Ollila, Ron Brooks, Frank Garlock,

Frank Hamrick, Jim and Patty Berg, Rand Hummel, Ken and Mardi Collier, Steve Pettit, Tom and Regina Farrell, Carl and Debbie Herbster, Greg Mazak, Matt Herbster, and Jim Binney.

2. Serving the Local Church

Along with the family and civic authority, God instituted the local church. God established the local church as the pillar and ground of the truth, and THE WILDS would be out of order to fail to recognize that God's plan for this ministry makes it a servant to God's church made up of local bodies of believers. The congregations of the churches and the ministries of the churches comprise the greatest majority of campers who come to THE WILDS. The campers who come to THE WILDS will generally mirror the health of the local churches as they come to enjoy the programs and property of THE WILDS. It is from the churches that we receive our greatest accountability, and it is the privilege of THE WILDS to be a partner with them to strengthen the spiritual lives of young people and adults.

From the very beginning of the ministry, several local church ministries have faithfully partnered with THE WILDS. As the ministry has grown, many more have joined and added their encouragement to keep it energized and running. Among the longtime Sustainers of twenty-five years or more are Hampton Park Baptist in Greenville, South Carolina, Heritage Bible Church in Greer, South Carolina, and Friendship Baptist in Raleigh, North Carolina. Each one of these, plus scores of other churches, deserves our deepest thanks for making THE WILDS their camp ministry.

3. Refreshing Enjoyment Life in Christ

Campers often describe coming to THE WILDS like enjoying a little taste of heaven. It is certainly not heaven; however, the joy and peace that comes when a group of people know Christ and delight to serve Him adds refreshment, zest, and encouragement to the

Christian life. A smile, a greeting, the catching of an eye, a song, a sense of humor, positive expressions of love, contentment with the work, genuine thankfulness, fellowship with one another, and appreciation for a brother or sister in Christ all say to everyone on the campsite, *"By this shall all men know that ye are my disciples, if ye have love one to another."* Because there are so many staff and campers who desire to love and obey Him, this savor and relish for life becomes part of the atmosphere of the place. THE WILDS is one of the places where enjoyment of the Christian life is natural. It is an atmosphere brought about by the influence of the Holy Spirit who indwells each staff member and believer who comes to camp.

THE WILDS is one of the places where enjoyment of the Christian life is natural.

4. Christlike Servants

If you want to be like Jesus Christ—and every Christian should have that goal—then you have to be a servant. At THE WILDS there is a race for every staff member. The race is not for the place of notoriety, not the high place. The race is for the low place, the place where needs are recognized and met sacrificially. It is a race to be responsive to the will of others, and a race to be responsive to the needs of others. The attitude that pervades the campsite is found in Philippians 2:3–5: *"Let nothing be done through strife or vainglory; but in lowliness of mind let each esteem other better than themselves. Look not every man on his own things, but every man also on the things of others. Let this mind be in you, which was also in Christ Jesus."*

Christ's servants do the repetitive things that need to be done with a Christlike spirit. Being a servant, among a myriad of other things, might include giving a second helping with a smile, cleaning a bathhouse, weeding an out-of-the-way garden, creating a unique game or performing a zany skit, answering an often-asked question, holding an unhurried conversation, preaching a strong gospel message, dispensing a Band-Aid or daily medications, rescuing keys locked in a car, advising about the best way to do a craft, planning a delicious menu, preparing a special cappuccino, unplugging a toilet, setting a table, adding a dollop of whipped cream to the dessert, or comforting a homesick camper. It means "laying aside the crown, picking up a towel, and washing dirty feet" (that is, meeting the most apparent need). There is no higher calling than being the servant of the greatest Servant who ever lived.

It would be impossible to list the servants of Christ who year after year have served cheerfully and at great sacrifice. Every year the roll of servants gets longer and longer as staff members and volunteers give their best for the glory of God at THE WILDS. A great reward will be received on that great day, and the impact will be surprising.

5. Committed to Excellence

At THE WILDS it is all about serving a God who is excellent in every way. Serving an excellent God requires that everything that is done for Him be done in keeping with His character, which means with excellence! If anything is done well, it is only mirroring and copying the One who is excellent. Regularly campers and visitors are giving testimony to the excellence of God by saying such things as, "I can't get over how organized this place is." "Everything is done with such quality." "It's so clean." "We've just never been to a place like this."

Being even a pitiful copy of the excellence of God means paying close attention to such things as the cleanliness of the buildings, the prompt beginning of each event and program, the proper repair of equipment and buildings, the uniform look of the staff, the beauty of the landscaping, the written philosophy for all to see, the organization of the registration and check-in, the light bulbs that work, the hot water that comes out hot, the music that was rehearsed and joyful, the brochures which were colorful and accurate, the chairs and plates that were aligned, the food that was delicious and plenteous, the messages which were prepared and enthusiastically preached, the counselors who were prepared to help, and a thousand other things were neatly arranged and cared for. The whole place seems to say, "We were expecting you!" It is a privilege to serve an excellent God for more than forty years. Although mistakes and oversights occur, the spirit of THE WILDS is one of excellence, for God has always been excellent and unfailing in His help towards this ministry.

6. Atmosphere Conducive to Spiritual Growth

What if one had the opportunity to set up an atmosphere wherein every detail is set to please God rather than dishonor Him? That is the challenge to THE WILDS every day. The opportunity is there to eliminate some of the distractions of which God would not approve, such as certain activities, jokes, worldly media offerings, and themes and associations that do not give the right opinion of God and His character. Wholesome activities are added into the mix in their place to bring glory to Him. Even though staff and campers battle the flesh every day, it is so refreshing to come to a place where forethought goes into what is allowed to be part of the atmosphere of camp.

It is a great privilege to search for, approve of, and encourage those things which God has created to glorify Himself. God delights in music, modesty, preaching, friendships, safe surroundings, godly role models, encouragement, edifying reading material, wholesome activities, and themes that build campers up in the faith. It is a privilege to be in an atmosphere where these God-pleasing elements are included in the daily schedule as much as possible. It is a selective atmosphere conducive to taking the next step of spiritual growth.

"Lord Jesus, please make these things true of THE WILDS until You come for Your children."

In Their Own WORDS

We have been coming to THE WILDS for over twenty years. Much has changed during those twenty years: hairlines receding, waistlines expanding, and longer waiting lines for registration, but the spirit of THE WILDS is intact and remains unchanged. The Lord is still honored and lives are still being changed! This is a blessing and is not to be taken lightly as many ministries have come and gone. We are grateful for your sweet spirit and excellent example. Thank you for everything you do for God and others.

—Sponsor

I want to take a minute and share with you some the blessing that we are reaping because of the sowing that was done at THE WILDS. One of our young ladies who was a camper at THE WILDS is now faithfully serving the Lord on the mission field in China. We had a young man who grew up coldhearted and running away from God, and it was at THE WILDS that he came to know Christ as his Savior. He went into the military, married, and is now home counting the blessings of the Lord in his life. Another girl is now on her way to Brazil after serving a summer at camp as a waitress. The list goes on and on of those serving the Lord because of the impact that the camp has had on their lives. Dr. Hay, THE WILDS will always hold a special place in the heart of this pastor and congregation for its faithfulness to the Word and the impact that it has made upon our people.

—Pastor

EPILOGUE

BY KEN HAY

WHETHER THEREFORE YE EAT, OR DRINK,

OR WHATSOEVER YE DO, DO ALL TO THE GLORY OF GOD.

1 CORINTHIANS 10:31

It is my prayer, and the desire of THE WILDS entire staff and board of directors, that by your reading this history of THE WILDS Camp and Conference Center, your thoughts will be directed to the greatness of our God. 1 Corinthians 10:31 should not be simply a passage of Scripture to recite, but rather a principle to be lived out daily in each of our lives. I also pray that the core values given in Chapter 15 will truly be evident in what we have been, what we are, and what we will be until the Lord comes to take His bride to glory. May God preserve our mission that is succinctly stated in the beginning pages of this book, and may it never be compromised by present or future staff.

It is usually true that God uses a few people to get a ministry started, but it takes many godly, faithful, and loyal people to keep it going. I have said facetiously on occasion that it seems to be easier to start a ministry than to keep it going. The truth of that statement has been relieved by the outstanding team of servants God has raised up to perpetuate our ministry. One youth leader wrote that he had been to many camps that had great preaching, beautiful campsites, and exciting programs, but he had never been to a camp that had so many godly servants to minister to him and his teens. He attributed the long-lasting results he has observed in his teens' lives to the serving staff. Campers regularly comment that although they had a great time enjoying the activities, it was the preaching and the staff that made the difference. As you read the testimonies that are at the end of each chapter and others given in appendix B, you will understand more how God has used our people for the furtherance of His glory.

I would be remiss if I didn't mention some of the people God used to make this ministry happen. First and foremost is my wife, Diane. She has backed me and the ministry one hundred percent, even though she was a professor at Bob Jones University, the busy housewife and mother of our three daughters, and the original Food Service Manager at the camp. Each weekend in the early days, she would pack up the children, order and pick up the food, work all weekend, and then report to the classroom on Monday at 8:00 a.m. She has stood beside me and the ministry through thick and thin. Sharing this very taxing schedule in the early days were also Jerry Sprout and Marsha Farr Van Steenburgh. Only eternity will reveal their impact on the campers and staff.

The charter members of our board of directors, Walt Fremont, Walt Rumminger, Walt Handford, Bob Jones III (How did a Bob get in there with all those Walt's?), Joe Henson, and Carl Blyth spent hours meeting in order to help determine our direction and master planning. We called our plan, "Master Planning the Master's Plan" (see appendix E). How grateful I am for the guidance of these and many others. My educational background was in Bible and ministry, not business. If it had not been for the wisdom and, may I say, patience and business acumen of Bob Stoner and John Brausch, I wonder where we would be financially.

I realize the risk of naming names, and there are scores of faithful servants who have made a significant contribution to the success of the ministry, but I must give thanks to God for calling Ken Collier to be a lifetime partner in ministry. His humble, godly, servant leadership has tempered my "prophet mindset" and has been the source of producing numerous other servants along the way. He, along with Dick Reid, has been my main source of counsel in these last several years.

I am always in awe when I have the privilege to stand before a group of people at a banquet or in a church which feels that THE WILDS is their camp. They are friends that pray, give, come to conferences, and support us in many other ways. This is one of the thrills of the ministry that never ceases to amaze me. Hardly a day passes that we will not hear of a camper who trusted Christ as his or her Savior, who made a very important decision that changed his or her life, or who yielded to the call of God for full-time vocational Christian service. This is very humbling, but very encouraging, to think that God would bless in so many wonderful ways.

All we can say is "To God be the glory, great things He has done."

Appendix A

Joel and Jo Ann Brighton's Testimony

Our relationship with THE WILDS is one which could only have been scripted by God. We first heard of the camp while attending Trinity Baptist Church in Concord, New Hampshire, then pastored by Dr. Chuck Phelps. After moving to North Carolina in 2003, Dr. Phelps invited us to participate in a pastor's conference at THE WILDS, giving our legal perspective on church ministries. We enjoyed our weekend there and were later able to return with our children for family camps and couples' conferences.

On June 20, 2005 while Joel was driving our two oldest children to Junior Boot Camp, a driver crossed the center lane only about five miles from camp, hitting our van head-on and critically injuring everyone. Joel broke his neck and was initially transported to the hospital in Brevard, then later moved to the trauma center in Greenville, South Carolina, where Casey and CJ had been airlifted and treated for head, facial, abdominal, and orthopedic injuries. God used many of the camp staff to minister to Joel and the children as well as to Jo Ann who was hours away at the time of the accident.

Looking back, we now view that "accident" as part of God's amazing plan to knit our lives together with THE WILDS in a special way, and we became forever bonded through having shared a time of tragedy together. The years to follow brought many more surgeries and hospitalizations, and all the camp staff soon became part of our family, bearing our burdens and upholding us in prayer. Their music carried us through many hospitalizations and pointed us to the promises of God, even opening up doors to give testimony to our great God during those bleak days.

Due to ongoing medical needs, we were unable to return to THE WILDS until the spring of 2006 when the staff invited us to a community open house. And it was later that summer, while our family was attending a family camp, that the Lord laid it on our hearts to assist with the writing of the history of THE WILDS. After discussing the project with Dr. Hay, we set a goal to have this book ready for the fortieth anniversary of the camp.

We share our story only because it testifies of the providence of a kind and loving God who truly does work all things together for the good of those who love Him. Little did we know on the day of our "accident" that we would one day collaborate with THE WILDS in telling their story. God gave us the privilege of witnessing firsthand the true calling of THE WILDS. We are so thankful for the impact this ministry has had not only on our family, but also on the lives of so many others we were privileged to interview while compiling the material for this book. We are only one family among a half million other campers that THE WILDS has impacted. Only God could have orchestrated this amazing story! Only God's power could have reached so many lives in just forty short years! Only God deserves all the glory forever!

Humbled to have a part in this project,
Joel and Jo Ann Brighton
Associate Editors/Authors of *All to the Glory of God*

Appendix B
In Their Own Words

I was a junior in college . . . no longer the frightened college rookie, and sort of feeling like I had this whole academia thing pretty much under control. That's when I started hearing the buzz. THE WILDS! What? Where? Who *are* these people incessantly buzzing about their amazing summer working at THE WILDS? They seemed to share a strong and substantial bond that I admired, yet they were friendly and warm to everyone. I saw them as effervescent and their enthusiasm just a bit contagious. Yes, I was intrigued, but not yet so sure I was ready to be "infected."

It soon hit closer to home when my dorm supervisor, Brenda Ball, started recruiting one of my best friends, Libby McGhee (Woodworth). Before I knew it, I was sort of riding Libby's coattails onto the summer staff of THE WILDS. How did this happen? What am I in for?! I like challenges, but I've always been a little apprehensive about new places and significant life changes. So, as reluctant and fearful as I was, I eventually caught THE WILDS bug . . . and I can tell you that the Lord certainly used THE WILDS to change my life.

I ended up counseling at THE WILDS for seven straight summers, three as a counselor and four as a lead counselor. And now I'm privileged to serve on the board as well. This place is huge in my life, because God did huge things *in* my life in this place. And He's doing huge things in the lives of my three sons now as well. I hadn't fathomed the gratitude I would feel as a parent upon seeing my own sons' solid and steady growth as a result of their time at THE WILDS.

What you actually take home with you from THE WILDS will be less about THE WILDS and much, much more about Christ Himself. He is the Focus; it is *not* THE WILDS that is special or meaningful or powerful; it is the God of THE WILDS that is all of these things! And more! So much more that you'll want a lifetime of *"continuing in the things that thou hast learned"* to know Him and serve Him better. And *that* is the message you will hear, you will see, you will live . . . when you're at this camp!

Kathy Stahlman Hildebrand
Snellville, Georgia

Though without official nexus, Bob Jones University and THE WILDS have a symbiotic relationship that is mutually treasured—and for which we each thank God. I was privileged to be among the handful who assembled that history-making day when the first spade of mountain dirt was turned. Into that shovel-sized indentation a seed of vision and faith was placed, from which has grown a camping ministry of God-ordained size and influence which none of us who stood there on that occasion could have envisioned.

THE WILDS is the Lord's doing, *"and it is marvelous in our eyes"* (Mark 12:11).

The great majority of our students have souls that were imprinted by the Word at THE WILDS prior to their enrollment here. In addition, THE WILDS becomes a summer laboratory for training our students in sacrificial ministry as members of its summer staff.

These are great days to serve the Lord Jesus Christ, and I'm glad we can serve Him together!

Dr. Bob Jones III, Chancellor
Bob Jones University
Greenville, South Carolina

When my wife, Patty, and I were first married, we were attending a church that regularly emphasized attending men's, women's, and couples' retreats at THE WILDS. I was still a student, and we really couldn't afford to attend couples' conferences, but the Lord always provided the means to do so. We made it a regular practice every year, and God used THE WILDS, along with the preaching of our local church, to help us start our marriage out on biblical grounds. Dr. Fremont and so many others ministered to us in those early years.

It has been our privilege since 1981 to be a part of the ministry of THE WILDS in various capacities. We praise God for the impact it has had upon our own lives and the lives of our children, all of whom spent their summers on staff. When they were growing up, they loved THE WILDS so much that we often joked that if they ever ran away from home, they would run to THE WILDS.

It is a great joy to us to be able to pass on to another generation of couples at THE WILDS those things that God taught us as a young couple in the very same place.

Dr. Jim Berg, Dean of Students
Bob Jones University
Greenville, South Carolina

THE WILDS Christian Camp is a miracle! As you read *All to the Glory of God*, you will trace God's hand through forty years of exciting and Christ-exalting camp ministry. You will understand how the biblical philosophy of founder, Dr. Ken Hay, permeates every aspect of the camp. The works of God recorded in this book will thrill your soul. You will glorify God for what He has done and is still doing at THE WILDS.

Dr. Tom Farrell, Evangelist
Tom Farrell Ministries
Independence, Missouri

While I was at camp this past week, I decided to watch the counselors more than I had in the past. The ministry that they have is a very important one and one that I know is a sacrifice. As I watched them in action, I thought to myself that as my own children grow older, these are the kinds of people I want as role models for them. I wish that I had been able to attend a place like THE WILDS when I was growing up.

Youth pastor

Thank you for the blessing and encouragement you were to our family this past week. I have been coming to THE WILDS since 1970, first as a camper, then as a counselor, and now as an adult camper with my whole family. While my husband was talking to a staff member, I was outside the Snack Shop watching my little four-year-old play. I walked over to the bench overlooking the Ballfield, and I remembered chasing the Bigball all over the field below. The Lord had used THE WILDS to mold and shape many of the major decisions of my life and solidified my biblical standards and convictions. It is difficult to express how special and dear this place has become for our family.

Family camper

We have arrived home tonight after a wonderful weekend with "y'all" at THE WILDS. Thank you! We brought three new couples with us this year, and they were powerfully blessed by the speaker, the food, the fun, and the godly atmosphere of the camp. I know what appears to be easy and fun for us takes a lot of work and planning for you to implement. We want you to know you are appreciated.

Couples' Conference camper

Just thinking about THE WILDS brings back many special memories. I still have my camp songbook. I find myself singing THE WILDS camp song, *W–I–L–D–S*, to my children over and over again. Thank you for making a positive impact on my life and helping me to hand down a Christian heritage to my family.

Camper

I want to take a few minutes to thank you and your staff for the great week of camp my teens experienced. I have often wondered what made your place superior to other camps that I have known. I considered the *beauty* of the grounds, but other camps had scenic landscapes. I thought about your excellent *program*, but other camps had good programs. I thought about the great *preaching*, but other places had good preaching. As I noted the smiles and kind service rendered by your staff, I realized what made the difference. It was the *people*. Thank you for your great example.

Youth pastor

Last year's camp completely overhauled our youth group. It was the springboard that our teens needed to build unity, faithfulness, and compassion for each other.

Youth director

A rebellious teenager came to THE WILDS in 1974 and got right with God. That same person returned to THE WILDS in 1977 as a counselor, surrendering his life for full-time Christian service. Now twenty years later I am coming back as a sponsor bringing my teenage son for the first time. It is exciting watching God do a good work in my son's life.

Camper parent

Two weeks ago I had the privilege of financing a week of camp for my three grandchildren. I want to thank you for being the instruments God has used in making THE WILDS a powerful means of drawing young people to Christ. All three of my grandchildren wrote that they will never forget the week they spent there and that "camp was awesome."

Grandmother

I was a young Jewish man who was saved eight months before I joined the summer staff as a cook at THE WILDS in 1988. After I arrived, I quickly realized that my background was different from the "typical staff member's." From the first day and on throughout the summer, the head cook, Cal, helped me grow spiritually. He exercised godly patience with me because I was spiritually and emotionally immature. Through the example of the godly staff in the Dining Hall, I did grow and mature spiritually and socially. I am truly grateful that the Lord led me to THE WILDS.

Summer cook

I want you to know about the wonderful week of camp that our young ladies experienced. All of the girls were spiritually blessed and talked about those experiences all summer long. I want to thank you for all the effort and time you put forth in everything you do for the lives of young people. Our girls were impressed with the quality of the cabins, the food, as well as the activities and overall program.

Thank you! We want you to know that you are making a difference in the lives of teens and adults and we appreciate it.

Pastor

My first experience at THE WILDS was in the summer of 1973. I was thirteen years old and was excited to have my first experience of summer camp. It was the first time our church had gone to THE WILDS. It was such a great week that we came back the next summer of 1974.

In 1975 once again I came to camp and looked forward to the great activities and fun that we would have. I was highly disappointed when I was not placed in the cabin with my best two friends, but this was in God's plan. He knew I needed the walls broken down in my life. The two previous years I had made a decision to rededicate my life to the Lord, but the real decision that needed to be made was the decision of salvation.

I remember well the Tuesday night service. We were in the Fireplace Room, and I was sitting with the guys from my cabin in the balcony. Dr. Ken Hay preached that night on repentance. It was as if I was the only one in the room. God showed me plainly that I had never repented of my sin, and all my trying to do "good" was only my flesh, and this was why I kept failing. I went forward and was saved. It was August 12, 1975.

My friends and I attended the camp's personal evangelism classes and went soul winning on Thursday in Asheville, North Carolina. God was truly changing us. We came home and knew we needed to be witnesses. We made the decision to go soul winning each Tuesday evening. We also made the commitment to start each day of school with prayer together at our public high school. These decisions were kept through our high school years.

God later led me to a Christian college and into the youth ministry. I have had the privilege bringing teenagers to THE WILDS many times. I also have had the blessing of attending and speaking at the Youth Workers' Conferences. These conferences have challenged me time and time again to live for God. I am forever indebted to Dr. Hay and THE WILDS staff for the input they have had in my life, my family, and our young people. To God be the glory, great things He hath done.

Youth Pastor Tommy Stone

I found THE WILDS NewsLetter this morning and tears came to my eyes as I began replaying and rehearsing in my mind all that THE WILDS has done in my life.

I came to THE WILDS each summer from 1973–1977. As I look back, I can gauge my spiritual growth from year to year at THE WILDS. I made major decisions there that did stick with me, by the way. I remember a long, difficult discussion with a counselor about total surrender one summer. He didn't sugarcoat it either. I was giving God my all regardless of what that meant in the future.

I really learned to have meaningful quiet times with God there at THE WILDS. Being from the big city (Detroit suburbs), I will always cherish discussions with God on the bridge over the creek or on the hill overlooking the camp (observing hundreds of others doing the same). I remember spiritual discussions with my counselors outside the birdhouse cabins, really digging into what it would look like to walk with God when I got back home to the daily grind. To this day I remember his advice and that specific discussion and our prayer together there next to that cabin.

On a funnier note, I recall waking up to wacky songs, racing *up* the seventy-six steps in 1976 (I was one of the fastest that summer), and racing *down* the experimental water slide with kitchen soap on my rear end for speed—Ken Collier's idea. I admit, I was eager to try it. My older brother was there the year before developing the "mud slide" and we perfected the soon-to-be water slide. A few years later, one of the camp dogs jumped in front of me as I zoomed down the slide, and I hit him broadside. I enjoy telling people that I was hit by a dog on the Superslide.

Ken, Ken, and all the others there at THE WILDS, thanks so much for being in a place to be used by God as significant influences in my life. I look forward to visiting again soon.

Campus Pastor Don Pedde

I was the final guy added to the twenty men that originally worked at the camp the summer of 1969. It was providential that Dr. Hay came to my church on a Sunday evening and I heard about his vision and wanted to join him. Over the years, THE WILDS philosophy of ministry, attention to detail, and determination to do everything to the best of its ability, has been consistent. The ministry genuinely loves people no matter where they are in their "faith walk" and attempts to help them take the next step spiritually they need to take. That first summer launched me on the road to ministry that I've been involved in for forty years now. I appreciate Dr. Hay for his influence on my life and character.

Pastor Jerry Dean
former Program Director at
THE WILDS

I still remember standing there by the creek on the newly acquired property of THE WILDS, dedicating the land to the Lord. I wondered what God was going to do with our dreams, and if I'd still be around forty years from now to see the dreams realized. I also remember coming up the old unpaved road and getting flat tires on the car because of all the sticks and stones.

The first year we had only three weeks of camp. The services were held down in the basement of the Dining Hall, and the group singing was electrifying. The next year we had our meetings in the Fireplace Room in the Lodge. We had kids hanging out the windows and off the balcony. We could hardly breathe because the kids would come in directly from off the athletic field without having time to go clean up first.

It was the first summer of camp that I wrote the theme song for THE WILDS called, *Wilds, Wilds, Wilds.* The counselors would insert *work, work, work* in place of *Wilds, Wilds, Wilds.* I have such fond memories of those first years of camp. I am overwhelmed by all the young people that have been spiritually influenced by THE WILDS. I pray that THE WILDS will have many more years of service for our Lord.

Dr. Frank Garlock, President
Majesty Music
Greenville, South Carolina

God has placed within my heart a strong passion for pushing forward a major discipleship emphasis at Clearwater Christian College, a passion that was most fervently stirred through the ministry of THE WILDS. Through our high school and college years, Holly and I both had the opportunity to serve as summer staff members. Without a doubt, the greatest spiritual impact on our lives while at THE WILDS came through our interactions with men such as Doc Hay and Ken Collier. We were privileged to sit under their preaching and wise counsel; but more importantly, we were privileged to interact with them in everyday venues of life where they "preached" messages to us by their actions and reactions. We had the opportunity to observe them in peaceful situations and in stress-filled situations, in moments of intense fun and in moments of intense work. We had the opportunity to observe their families and their interactions with their wives and their children. We watched them closely, and we learned. We didn't observe perfect men, but we observed men who were lovers of a perfect God; and as lovers of a perfect God, they were servants of men. The Lord gave us the wonderful privilege of witnessing them sacrificially pouring their lives into others with a grace that only comes through a life that is centered on Christ. We observed many staff members who reflected the Lord Jesus Christ, and we praise God for them all. How thankful Holly and I are for a ministry that offered us such a clear demonstration of genuine servant leadership, and a ministry that daily reminded us to do everything for the glory of God!

Dr. Dick Stratton, President
Clearwater Christian College
Clearwater, Florida

It is a privilege for me to share some of the positive influences THE WILDS has had upon me, my family, and on our ministry at Tri-City Baptist Church in Kansas City. I could probably write a book myself about the various aspects that have impacted our lives.

I first visited THE WILDS in 1978 as an assistant pastor in charge of the Singles Class at Community Baptist Church in South Bend, Indiana. I was immediately impressed by the quality of the staff, the preaching, and the music.

As a parent, I was so thankful for the family emphasis at THE WILDS. Not only have the youth camps impacted my children and our church young people, but the couples' conferences and family camps have been life-changing for us as well. My wife and I will never forget the first couples' retreat we attended at THE WILDS. We had a canopy bed—bunk beds pushed together! At that retreat we made a commitment to pray together every night before we went to sleep. We have been doing that consistently since that time, and God has blessed and answered many prayers!

Our sons had the wonderful privilege of being campers for many summers in North Carolina and at THE WILDS of the Rockies. Matt's first camp experience was in the summer of 1981, when he was nine years old. He had a broken leg with a full-leg cast, but was encouraged to come anyway. His counselor, Jeff Craven, carried him up and down the multitude of steps! After years of being campers, our sons could not wait for the day they could serve on Operational Staff and then as counselors. Now our son, Matt and his wife, Julie, and their five children live and serve full-time at THE WILDS. What a wonderful place for them to raise their family! It is a great joy for us to see our family ministering at a place that has had such an impact in our lives as a family! We have had the blessing of hearing many great preachers at THE WILDS, and we have personally made many spiritual decisions there. It is humbling to now come and hear our sons preach at THE WILDS! God has used THE WILDS to help encourage our sons to be faithful servants of the Lord.

We will not know until we get to heaven the number of decisions that have been made at this camp and the number of people who have been impacted through its many ministries. However, I know one person, one family, and one church that have been greatly helped and strengthened spiritually because of THE WILDS Christian Camp and Conference Center. I praise God for the way He has used THE WILDS in my life and ministry—*all to the glory of God!* May *"the Lord be magnified!* (Psalm 40:16).

Dr. Carl Herbster, Pastor
Tri-City Ministries
Kansas City, Missouri

Appendix C
Tribute to Dr. Hay

As of December 31, 2006, Dr. Hay stepped aside as President and CEO of THE WILDS Christian Association, Inc. No, he did not retire or leave THE WILDS after thirty-nine years of ministry, but he felt it was time to place the daily operations of the ministry into the younger but capable hands of Ken Collier. Dr. Hay was elected Chairman of the Board, and his stepping down made it possible for him to have more input on corporate matters.

At the time of Dr. Hay's resignation, Ken Collier wrote this tribute about Dr. Hay:

> Ken Hay was always bigger than real life to me. He still is! He became my hero in the mid-1960s at little Christian Dells Bible Camp in the bustling "metro area" of Trinity, Alabama (as small as it sounds). Christian Dells was my growing-up camp and the place where God got hold of my heart again and again. There was something about the camp environment that made this young boy listen to God like he never had before. Each year, or every couple of years, we would have to break in a new camp director at Christian Dells. When this fellow, Ken Hay, came to direct, it was pretty obvious there was a new sheriff in town. This guy could knock a softball into oblivion and shoot a leathery-soft hook shot that Wilt and Shaq would love. For all the intensity of sports, his passion was for his God. His mission was for me and my friends to learn to serve God with our lives! He was serious about daily living for Christ. He

was serious about turning from sin. He was serious about this personal devotions thing called "God & I Time." I was blown away and couldn't ignore or get away from his life message of "all to the glory of God." It was impossible to ignore the man or his Christ. He hasn't changed an iota. Well, maybe the softball doesn't go as far and the hook shot doesn't float as well, but, unlike me, he is still playing those games. However, the really important things in his life have never diminished. So I got myself a new hero that summer long ago. This hero was instrumental in guiding me to my all-time Hero, Jesus Christ. It all happened at a camp. It made sense that when I saw Ken Hay's name on the marquee as introducing a new camp called THE WILDS at a late-afternoon meeting on the campus of Bob Jones University in 1968, I just had to be there. As an eighteen-year-old freshman, I was spellbound as I heard Ken Hay's dream, and I asked God to somehow make me a part of it. I didn't even understand that for which I was praying. God understood and by supernatural grace, and who knows how many other amazing miracles, actually answered my prayer! I still do not understand, nor do I feel in the least worthy to serve God at THE WILDS. Four decades have literally raced along under the leadership of Ken Hay. It just seems natural and right for him to be at the helm.

Now comes that intruding and uncomfortable word, *transition*. I ran across a definition for this interloper. It reads: "a change from one place, state, or stage to another." You can rightly say that THE WILDS is in transition. The fact that Ken Hay will, for the first time in over thirty-nine years, not be the Executive Director or President of THE WILDS is one whale of a change of status. We are in a new stage of life. Humanly speaking, I don't like it one bit. Ken Hay will always be "Mr. WILDS," even though he has thoroughly indoctrinated every staff member that "it is not personality, but biblical philosophy" that wins the day. Because he has preached "biblical philosophy, not personality," we know what we need to do. We are so thankful God brought the man and the dream together when He burdened Ken Hay, and such men as Joe Henson, Walt Fremont, and Carl Blyth, to found a camp in the Southeast. Handing over the reins is very consistent with his biblical philosophy. Even so, it's hard to imagine that the time is now and that we are the ones to pick up the mantle. For my part, I know that this 5-foot, 8-inch Christian does not measure up to that 6-foot, 3-inch Christian in any regard—either physically, mentally, or spiritually. But for the Lord's help, it would be overwhelming. However, we are all thrilled that Ken Hay remains a strong, healthy, steadying influence at THE WILDS. His cell phone is still on his belt, his office light is on, and his many talents place him in the vital position of Chairman of the Board. We are content to know that what Ken Hay and the board are doing is being done in a forward-looking, orderly way. This is comforting to everyone, I'm sure. Like so many other men on THE WILDS staff, and in other ministries around the country and world, Ken Hay's voice is in my mind and his life is in my heart. He has carried the responsibilities of founder, director, executive, president, and, as he often says, "chief cook and bottle washer" with absolute dignity and integrity. He has thrown in the responsibility of "beloved father" in the mix. He will, undoubtedly, bring the board and the staff together in new ways that will glorify

God. Is there anyone who would say that Ken Hay has not done an excellent and inspiring job running THE WILDS? His influence will not end. As near as I can tell, it's taking five or six men to replace him in his various functions. Will you pray for these men as we carry the torch? There is hardly a day when we fail to hear of a life that was changed by God's grace at THE WILDS. Can you imagine what it must be like for Ken and Diane Hay to look back and to realize just a portion of what God has done in lives from the ministry born in their hearts long ago? The whole miracle of THE WILDS, and their part in it, is . . . well . . . much bigger than life!

Appendix D

TRIBUTE TO COACH ROYER FROM DR. HAY

When the University of Maryland football team came to South Carolina to play Clemson University, Mike Greene had the football defensive backfield coach from Maryland, H. Lee "Rock" Royer, speak at an afterglow activity for the church young people. Having heard the results, I called the University of Maryland Athletic Department and contacted Coach Royer. After I talked with him on the phone for about five seconds, I felt like I had known this man all my life. He had the most contagious personality of any man I had ever met. I scheduled him to speak that summer at our camp. When I called a little later to confirm his speaking, I found that he was no longer at the University of Maryland, but had transferred to the U.S. Naval Academy in Annapolis, Maryland, as the Defensive Coordinator for the football team. When I confirmed his coming, I immediately set the wheels in motion to have an Army-Navy week that summer. Even though we already had another theme the rest of the weeks, we had Coach Royer head up the Navy team and Major Ron Brooks lead the Army team. It was during that first week of Army-Navy camp that the organized cheering really became big at THE WILDS. The competition became very fierce between the Army and the Navy. Coach would stand on top of the trashcan out in front of the Dining Hall leading cheers for the Navy. Of course, Ron Brooks was not to be outdone, and he would have his own platform. We learned later that Coach Royer ate the pre-shift meal with the staff so he did not have to worry about eating during the camper meals. He would walk around the Dining Hall working up the "sailors." We finally had to make a rule that the campers could not cheer for the first twenty minutes of the meal because the kids would be in the aisles cheering instead of eating. They would be knocking food off the tables, hinder the waitresses from their work, and cause general chaos. However, even with the "no-cheer" rule, Coach would periodically walk by the microphone and whisper as he walked by, "Go Navy!" and the place would erupt. Major Ron Brooks had managed to schedule a helicopter to come in from Fort Gordon, and of course that created quite a stir and excitement for the Army team. Then, in poking fun at Coach Royer, Major Brooks bought Coach a little toy boat that had a horn that tooted, obviously a big contrast between the real helicopter and the little toy boat. Coach Royer, however, was able to take that boat and make it a mascot and a rallying point for the Navy team.

Needless to say, we initiated an Army-Navy flag football game on the campsite, and before the game, we had a big parade. The teams made floats out of two of the vehicles that we had on the campsite. One vehicle was an old 1949 Ford, as I recall. The other was a vehicle we called "Manna," which means "we know not from whence it cometh." The campers, in making the Ford into a float, had stuffed paper in the grill. As they were driving it down the hill to the Ballfield, the engine heated up and steam was pouring out of the radiator. Behind these floats was a kazoo band led by Frank Garlock, featuring the staff and the campers. Leading the band was a drum major, and I happened to be the one elected for that position. They had rescued a carpet cardboard roll. The staff put rags on each end, and Tom Hill soaked the rags generously with kerosene. I had a flaming baton about fifteen feet long. As I was twirling it around, the fire came up the tube itself, and it became very hot. I obviously had to discard it in a hurry or else the consequence would have been disastrous. We have pictures in our archives of these floats, the drum major, and the kazoo band. That was the first—and last—time that Ken Hay was a drum major!

Coach's famous message was "The Three Types of People." His text was from Revelation 3, describing the church at Laodicea. He would verbally paint a picture of three types: one was the spiritual man, one was the natural man, and the other was the lukewarm or cool man. He would talk about the ten percent who were hot for God, the ten percent who were cold to the things of God, and the eighty percent who were the shoulder shruggers. He would preach this message at least one time whenever he was at THE WILDS, and it always challenged the listeners to greater service for the Lord. During Army-Navy week in the summer of 1973, we produced a sixteen-millimeter public relations film which featured Coach Royer. He gave excerpts of that message that we have for our archives. If I remember right, we filmed his scene about 3:00 a.m. the last night of camp. We woke him up from sleep, but he still had the enthusiasm that only Coach Royer could exude.

Earlier, Coach Royer's life was totally changed while being part of a sports camp at Word of Life camp in New York State. He said that he would go to an early-morning prayer meeting because it was expected of him, but he was usually half asleep. He was impacted by the sincere and enthusiastic devotion and prayer to God these men exhibited. He realized that the men had already spent much time with God even before that prayer meeting. This experience turned Coach around from just being a nominal Christian to a dynamic witness for Christ. When he was at the University of Maryland, basketball Coach Lefty Driesell started calling him "Coach Born Again" because every time Coach saw Lefty Driesell, he would ask him when he was going to get born again. Coach witnessed to everyone. I remember him witnessing to teenagers at the Big Orange restaurant on South Pleasantburg Drive in Greenville, South Carolina. It was a Friday night after one of the local football games and the place was wall-to-wall teenagers. To my disgrace, I said, "Let's get our orange juice and go outside because it is so noisy in here." But Coach had found a mission field. He was passing out tracts to the students sitting at the booths and tables and witnessing to them. When the players found out he was a college football coach, they came right up to him. He asked the players what position they played, how they did in the game, and other sports questions. Then he let them know what was greater than winning a football game: being born again. On another occasion I remember taking him to the doughnut shop that was in the Lake Forest Shopping Center. He asked the man behind the counter if he was born again. The man said he was subbing for his daughter that day and was a retired Baptist preacher. Coach got so excited to find a born-again believer that he jumped up on the counter and was patting this guy on the back saying, "Praise the Lord! Isn't it great to be born again?!" Needless to say, the doughnuts were flying!

Coach said that he liked to sit in the middle seat on an airplane right over the wing. Of course, no one liked to sit in the middle seat, but Coach did. (This was before they assigned seats on most of the flights.) He would try to sit next to someone who had a window seat. After they were airborne, he would look out the window and say, "Look at that wing. It's kind of flopping, isn't it? What happens if it breaks off? Have you been born again?"

At the 1972 Christmas camp, we had approximately three hundred young people in attendance. The Fireplace Room was completely jammed with teenagers and adults, both downstairs and the balcony. The young people sat on the edge of the balcony with their feet dangling. The campers came in from outside and would bang their feet against the edge of the balcony. The teens sitting below would experience a shower of . . . well . . . dirt. At any rate we had the first service during that Christmas camp, and Coach Royer, who was the speaker, was not in the room. Steve López was leading the music, and since we had already introduced Coach Royer during the orientation time, Steve announced that after the next song, Coach was coming to speak. I made a beeline to E-10 in the Lodge where Coach was staying. When I walked into the room, he was on his knees praying. I told him he was to speak as soon as the song was over. He said he could not go out to preach because he was backslidden, and he asked me to pray for him. I argued that he needed to go, but he insisted that I pray for him. I told him I would make a deal with him. I would pray, and he would go preach. Again he told me he could not go. So I prayed a brief prayer, and Coach left the room. I remember him standing up on the fireplace hearth telling the campers he was sorry he was late getting there, but that he had come to camp backslidden. "You see," he said, "I have not witnessed to anybody for three days." What an impact that made on all of the staff and campers. According to Coach's standard, many of us certainly were in a backslidden condition. The thing that bothered me was not so much the three days, but many may have gone three weeks, three months, or even three years without witnessing. What an impact Coach made on our camp in the three short years that he ministered to us.

Because he spoke at the camp, he was asked to speak at many churches and youth groups and had a great impact before God took him home to Himself. In fact he had John 3:3 on the side of a Cherokee 6 airplane that he bought and was learning to fly. On November 20, 1973, he flew out of Milton, Florida, and Dayton Hobbs, who pastors a church there, questioned whether Coach should fly because of the weather. Coach felt he had it under control, but he flew into tornadic winds that broke the struts off of his plane, and he crashed in Evergreen, Alabama. Coach Royer went to be with the Savior he served so enthusiastically.

At that time we were building the Activity Center on the north side of the Ballfield, and we dedicated it to a great man, a coach, and a preacher, and called it the H. Lee "Rock" Royer Activity Center.

Appendix D

THE HEMLOCK HILLS CHRISTIAN ASSOCIATION, INC. PRESENTS THE WILDS MASTER PLAN

(REPRODUCED VERBATIM FROM THE DOCUMENT WRITTEN EARLY IN 1970).

The Board of Trustees spent many hours before any development was actually done at *The Wilds Camp* and Conference Center. In order to know exactly the direction which the organization was headed as far as the buildings and land development were concerned, we now submit a revised Master Plan, keeping in mind the intent of the original founders of the organization.

MASTER PLAN

The purpose for constructing *The Wilds* Camp and Conference Center is to provide year-round Christian camping that reaches the entire family. The buildings that are constructed and the various campsites that are developed are geared to most effectively reaching the particular age groups intended. This camp program is to work as an arm of the local church and as an educational tool of the Christian school to use the out-of-doors to evangelize, edify, and educate. It is our feeling that God's timing is perfect as we follow His will and that He will direct us and guide us in the proper timing for the fulfillment of these plans that are yet future. The camping field is wide open for progress, the campsite is adequate to expand, and the camp staff is eager to branch out!

Phase I (Already Completed)

Land improvements

General—The main road into the camp is developed, the 20-acre athletic field cleared, roads to the various waterfalls opened, 10-acre lake built with a 40-foot high dam. Two softball fields, a football field, a soccer field, plus 2 badminton courts, 2 volleyball courts, and a basketball court have been developed on the athletic field. Also, a rifle range and archery range are in operation. A picnic area and garden spots are located at strategic places.

Water Supply—Two 300 foot wells supply the water for the main camp. These wells have enclosed well houses and pump water to a 10,000 gallon storage tank. This storage tank, which has an adjoining pumphouse, pumps the water to the various areas. There is a separate well and pumphouse for the 2 caretakers' homes.

Sewer Disposal—An aero-flo treatment plant is utilized to take care of the sewerage from the dining room and lodge, and is sized to take care of other buildings that will be built at the main camp area. Three septic tanks are provided for the 9 A-Frame dwelling and one for each of the bathhouses in the 4 cabin areas.

Electrical—The main source of electricity is supplied by the REA, however, the camp has purchased all the transformers and line within the actual camp area. All the lines within our property are underground as are the communications' systems to the various areas at the campsite. The camp is total electrical for cooking, heating, and air-conditioning.

Buildings

Lodge—21,000 square feet building with 50-foot square fireplace room, snack shop, bookstore, recreation room, offices, and 21 motel rooms. These motel rooms double as dormitory rooms for winter camping until further facilities can be built.

Dining Room—14,000 square feet of floor space to be able to seat 500 people at one time. This building is designed for expansion by adding approximately 50 more feet to the west end. The kitchen is equipped to feed 1,300 people in order to cater to outpost camps to be built later. Food storage is supplied on the ground floor along with temporary housing for our laundry facilities. A large 50' x 75' storeroom is presently being used for a meeting hall seating 400 people at a time.

Caretakers' Facilities—Two homes built at the entrance of the camp to provide housing for permanent residents at the camp. These are three-bedroom homes with a full basement.

Cabins—46 cabins (birdhouses) each housing 8 people with a bathhouse for each 10 cabins at the boys' cabin areas and for each 13 cabins at the girls' cabin areas. This provides for 322 campers plus 46 counselors.

Equipment Shed—A birdhouse cabin has been modified to provide for storage of athletic equipment.

A-Frame Dwellings—Seven two-bedroom dwellings and two three-bedroom dwellings constructed for rental purposes, for staff housing where children are involved, for utilization in couples' camps. Most of these have been donated by individuals who, because of their gift for such a dwelling, are invited by the camp administration to use this facility free of charge during the winter months.

Warehouse—A 30' x 60' metal building located near the caretakers' homes for storage, automotive repair, and wood shop.

Phase II

Three buildings are proposed for Phase II—a Dormitory, Activity Center, and an addition to the Dining Room.

Dormitory—This building is to be a two-story structure with 36 rooms and 8 restroom facilities. The primary function is to provide adequate housing for winter camping, summer overflow, and adult housing. This facility will allow us to become involved more in couples' camps and family camping. It will house 36 couples or families providing adequate restrooms. When campers are utilizing the facility, the girls have two stories on one end and the boys, two stories on the other. On the ground floor of this facility, which is to be built on the edge of the ballfield to the left of the main steps leading from the lodge, will be the craft shop. (Completed December 15, 1974.)

Activity Center—This building, named in honor of Coach H. Lee "Rock" Royer, will be called the ROYER MEMORIAL ACTIVITY CENTER. It will double as the main preaching center as well as an indoor recreation site, and 850 people could be seated for sessions in this building. It is designed to have to cross-court basketball courts and one full-length one. There will be restrooms attached to it. The ultimate goal is to build in shower rooms and to provide for a second story above them for ping pong tables, wrestling mats, etc. This building will be heated for year-round use.

Addition to Dining Room—This building is to house the walk-in freezer and cooler that have been donated to *The Wilds*. Along with covering for these items, there will be a 12' x 18' storeroom and a 12' x 7' office for the food service manager and dietician. The storage inside the back entrance to the dining room will be removed, the door changed to the outside wall, and five more tables added. This will provide for 40 more seats.

Phase III

Tent and Trailer Facility—Facilities to be located at the head of the lake in the area commonly called the Rabbit Patch. A central bathhouse is to be built along with electrical and water outlets to various camping positions in this area. This facility should be able to adequately take care of approximately 30 recreational vehicles plus 10 to 15 tent sites.

Indian Village—In order to house 200 more campers, it is the plan to build an authentic Cherokee Indian Village. This village will involve Indian-style dwellings for cabins, a multi-purpose building for dining room, crafts, and meeting rooms. An amphi-theatre and swimming pool is also planned. Its ultimate use would be for junior campers in the future, however, it will be utilized immediately for junior highs and senior highs as well. It is intended that this facility will not be winterized but will be utilized for summer camping.

Bridge to Girls' Cabin Area—This is to replace the present log bridge in order to provide safe passage at all times. The present bridge is inundated when rain storms appear. Therefore, the new bridge must be raised.

Tennis Courts—To be constructed and fenced in on present ball field.

Phase IV

Enclosed Amphitheatre—This building would be located on what we presently call the graveyard, which is northwest of the dining room on the opposite side of the road. This facility overlooks the valley and mountains to the north. It will be amphi-theatre style with a curved roof cover supported in the front by laminated beams in the form of a cross. This should be large enough to house 850 to 1,000 people.

FUTURE DEVELOPMENT

It is the ultimate goal of the Directors of Hemlock Hills Christian Association, Inc. to be able to provide year-round camping for all age groups. The main camp being a family camp and conference, the Indian Village for juniors, a Frontierland for junior highs, and an Olympic Village for senior highs. The high school camp is to be built on what is presently called High School Ridge. The Frontierland is to be built to the southeast of the campsite providing a complete motif for a western program, including horses. Each of these facilities is schedule to house approximately 250 campers plus staff.

OTHER FACILITIES to be built are as follows: (not listed in chronological order)

Classroom Building—To provide a permanent residence and meeting place for equipment used in the school camping program. Also, to provide for the development of a nature museum.

Chapel—Across from the lodge on the hill immediately above the creek, a chapel seating approximately 200 people to be built for utilization for special events and for smaller groups. This chapel is to be in A-Frame style having choir rooms and restroom facilities included.

Infirmary—This dwelling should be built in the main camp area near the lodge and dining room. It should provide a waiting room, treatment rooms, boys' in-patient room, girls' in-patient room, bathroom facilities for patients, and a nurse's quarters, complete with bath and rooms for a minimum of two nurses.

Laundry Facilities—To be built in the general area behind the dining room to provide for coin-operated washers and dryers space to allow for storage of linens, towel, etc. used in housekeeping.

Swimming Pools—Two large swimming pools to be built, one near the girls' cabinsite and one near the boys' cabinsite. These pools should be fenced with slides, diving boards, and wading pools. Bathhouse facilities should be provided for boys and girls' dressing rooms, baskets for checking clothes, and storage.

Gift Shop—A gift shop to be built in the general area of the lodge that will provide a complete bookstore facility for gifts, Christian books, and clothing.

Hotel—It is suggested that this hotel be called the HEMLOCK HOUSE and is to be built between the dining room and the lodge. It should be a multi-story building either in a U-shape with the front across the parking lot or in a square with a center court. It should have roughly 100 rooms plus a lobby and executive offices. As the Lord tarries and the camp expands, there is the prospect of the main offices and all the personnel involved moving to the campsite and having the central offices located in this hotel building. It may be necessary ultimately to build a separate office building for the year-round operation, and the business affairs of the organization.

Shelter—This building to be constructed on the knoll overlooking Inspiration Point. It should be an open shelter where people can go to meditate, can enjoy the beauty of that site, or to meet in small groups for counselor classes, Bible studies, etc.

Staff Housing—It is the goal of the camp to build on the campsite near the entrance numerous staff houses for permanent staff members. Beyond these, there are plans to develop areas on the east side of our property (Round Mountain side) where there will be leased properties for people to build permanent dwellings.

Airstrip—To be constructed on ridge in the northwest corner of the property. It will be a maximum of 3,000 feet.

Land Purchases—It is our desire to purchase the land north and west of the caretakers' homes that includes the land west and south of Frozen Creek Road.

Programming Possibilities

Christian School Camping—It is our goal to conduct school camping a minimum of 25 weeks a year.

Wilderness Camping—We desire to expand our Wilderness Camp to the entire summer for both boys and girls. This Wilderness Camp will not need any permanent dwellings, other than places to store equipment through the winter. A survival program with an emphasis on stress camping is the natural step beyond the Wilderness Camp.

Travel Camping—This, also, is a part of our future plans where campers would come to *The Wilds* for a week of inspiration and instruction and then go from there to various mission fields for missionary work or for canoe tripping through northern Minnesota, or Canada. There is the possibility of taking foreign trips with ski camps to Switzerland or tours to other areas of Europe and the mid-East. Having a boarding school for senior high young people is a real possibility for permanent use of our facility.

Senior Citizens Camps—Providing activities for retired persons that involves planned excursions as well as a Bible Conference setting.

Other uses and directions will become plain to us as we live with the present facilities and as God would open up other doors. We are not interested in just building buildings and developing a campsite, but we desire to see these facilities used to develop lives and see individuals, families, churches, and schools changed through the Gospel message that is proclaimed.

We want our Master Plan to truly be "a Master Plan of The Master's Plan."

Map of Original Site Plan

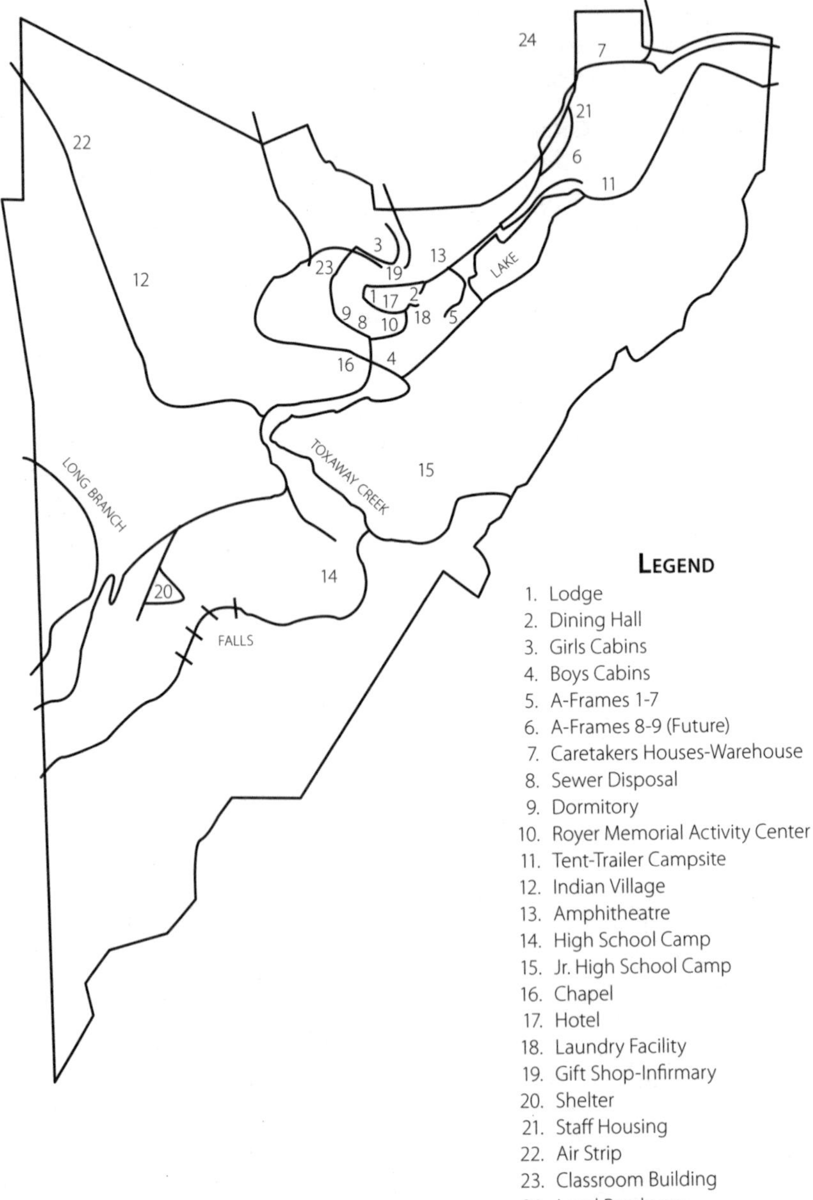
24
7
21
22
6
11
3
13
23
19
LAKE
12
1
17
2
9
8
10
18
5
16
4
LONG BRANCH
TOXAWAY CREEK
15
14
20
FALLS
Legend
1. Lodge
2. Dining Hall
3. Girls Cabins
4. Boys Cabins
5. A-Frames 1-7
6. A-Frames 8-9 (Future)
7. Caretakers Houses-Warehouse
8. Sewer Disposal
9. Dormitory
10. Royer Memorial Activity Center
11. Tent-Trailer Campsite
12. Indian Village
13. Amphitheatre
14. High School Camp
15. Jr. High School Camp
16. Chapel
17. Hotel
18. Laundry Facility
19. Gift Shop-Infirmary
20. Shelter
21. Staff Housing
22. Air Strip
23. Classroom Building
24. Land Purchases